F I R S T   T E E

ALSO BY JONATHAN ABRAHAMS:

ClubSmarts

FIRST TEE

JONATHAN ABRAHAMS

ILLUSTRATION BY BARRY ROSS

LYONS & BURFORD, PUBLISHERS

Printed in Montréal, Canada
Design by Kathy Kikkert
Typesetting and composition by Sam Sheng, CompuDesign

10 9 8 7 6 5 4 3 2 1

Library of Congress Cataloging-in-Publication Data
Abrahams, Jonathan.
First tee / Jonathan Abrahams.
p.   cm.
Includes index.
ISBN   1-55821-445-3
1. Golf.   I. Title.
GV965.A22   1996
796.352—dc20

CONTENTS

PREFACE VII

CHAPTER 1 WHERE IT ALL BEGAN · 1

CHAPTER 2 GETTING STARTED · 7

CHAPTER 3 THE GOLF COURSE · 15

CHAPTER 4 EQUIPMENT · 21

CHAPTER 5 BASIC TECHNIQUE · 37

CHAPTER 6 PUBLIC, PRIVATE, AND RESORT
COURSES · 61

CHAPTER 7 ETIQUETTE · 73

CHAPTER 8 IMPROVEMENT · 95

CHAPTER 9 HANDICAPS · 115

CHAPTER 10 GOLFING MINORITIES · 121

CHAPTER 11 THE ESSENTIAL GOLFER · 133

GLOSSARY · 145

INDEX · 155

PREFACE

I started playing golf because of Johnny Miller. When I was seven, he was the big superstar on tour. He had longish blond hair, like me, and was tall and thin, like my dad. I wanted to be just like him. But when I told my father I wanted to play, he just shook his head. "Golf is for really fat old men who smoke cigars and wear ugly clothes," he said.

"It is not," I protested. "Johnny Miller isn't fat, and he doesn't smoke cigars, and he doesn't wear—" At which point my father plopped a Sears catalog down in front of me and showed me a picture of Johnny Miller wearing a canary leisure suit. It was the mid-seventies, and I didn't know anything about endorsement contracts, but I could still recognize a fashion don't. "Well, he's not fat," I said under my breath.

Like any kid, I pestered Dad incessantly after that, and he finally relented, buying me a set of golf clubs for my eighth birthday. "Thanks," I said. "Let's go play."

And we did. Or we tried. When we arrived at the course, the man in the shop told us that our cutoff jeans weren't appropriate, and when I stood up on the first tee and whiffed twenty-one times before making contact, he came running out of the shop and told my father that he couldn't let us play, we weren't good enough and we'd hold up all the players behind us. Who, by the way, stood by on the first tee and laughed, one hand holding their big bellies, the other their Cubans.

In retrospect, it's a miracle I ever continued with the game, considering how bad that initial experience was. I'm not sure what brought me back. It's not like I had any fun that day: My father was justifiably angry and a bit embarrassed; I had been humiliated; and after we got banished to the driving range, my brother—who was just along for the ride—smacked shot after shot into the air while I continued to whiff. Was I a glutton for punishment? I don't think so, not at that age. I think the reason I didn't give up golf forever is that somewhere inside me, I sensed how great the game could be. That's the kind of foresight a child's optimism brings with it.

Whatever the reason, I went back the following week and whiffed only twice on the first tee before safely dribbling my ball somewhere out in the fairway. The man behind the counter stayed in the shop. And then, on my fourth shot, I swung mightily with my Chi Chi Rodriguez junior 5-iron and launched the ball into what seemed like orbit. And that, I can say with all honesty, was the best feeling I've ever had in my life. There was no turning back. I spent the rest of that summer discovering golf, sometimes with others, but mostly by myself.

My relationship with the game progressed in a manner typical of an obsessed youngster. I subscribed to every golf magazine I could, I got a job at the local golf course, and I began playing in junior tournaments. I became an equipment junkie, and by the time I joined my high school golf team as a freshman, I was doing my own club repairs and refinishing old persimmon woods. I went on to serve as captain of my high school and, later, college teams, but competition was never what golf was really about for me. I was in love with the entire game, from its history to course architecture to teaching the game; and so, upon graduation, it seemed only appropriate that I get a job with the publication that had been my textbook for all those years: *Golf Magazine.* Fifteen years after I got kicked off the first tee of my local course, golf had provided me with hours of enjoyment and a career to boot. And none of it would have happened if it weren't for my egoless eight-year-old heart.

Everybody who plays golf should be as lucky as I was, but few are. As we get older we become less and less willing to learn the hard way. Imagine an adult going to the golf course, being chastised about the clothes he was wearing, then hustled off the course—after he'd already started—because he wasn't good enough? That kind of experience would make all but the strongest of constitution (or most masochistic) run and hide from the game forever.

And that would be a shame. Because, as I have come to learn, my intuition was right on when I was eight: Golf is a great game. Even at its lowest levels it's athletics, science, artistry, and therapy wrapped up in one amazing package. It will introduce you to new people, let you see new places, and, to be sure, teach you a few things about yourself.

There are countless other reasons to love the game, too, which you will discover for yourself—as long as you don't run into the trouble along the way. There are a lot of pitfalls between the decision to try the game and making it a part of your life, and this book is designed to help you make that journey as pleasant as possible. Whatever reason you have for starting—you idolize Greg Norman, your boss wants you to play, there are a lot of available singles at your local course—is just fine. The desire to start is all you need. That's where this book comes in. It will guide you from that starting point of desire through all the early stages: learning the game, negotiating the golf course, buying equipment, and getting a taste of what the golf world is all about. Then, once you've read this book, golf itself will be your guide. Whenever it happens—just as it did for me when I hit that first 5-iron years ago—there will be no turning back.

Jonathan Abrahams
New York, New York

CHAPTER 1

WHERE IT ALL BEGAN

If *you look up* golf *in an encyclopedia, no doubt the entry will begin with a brief overview of the game's origins; after all, that's how encyclopedias do things. Look up* basketball *and you'll find its*

The Old Course at St. Andrews, Scotland, considered the birthplace of the modern game.

inventor, Dr. James Naismith, in the first paragraph. Turn to *foot-ball* and there will be a mention of the inaugural game between Rutgers and Princeton.

But does the kid who steps onto the playground to play hoops for the first time need to know about Naismith's efforts to find a winter sport for his students? Is it important that a freshman on a high school football team know Rutgers and Princeton played with twenty-five players on a side, and without forward passes? Not unless he's also writing a term paper. These facts, although perhaps interesting, have little bearing on how, or why, the modern games are played.

Not so with golf. In fact, every time you step onto a golf course to tee it up, your motives are directly related to the reasons for the game's creation. It's a lot more than trying to hit a tiny white ball into a hole.

Although there's evidence that an early form of golf was played by the Dutch as early as the twelfth century, Scotland is recognized as its birthplace, because it was there that the game's most significant development occurred.

In 1744, the Honourable Company of Edinburgh Golfers convened for the first time. It's credited with being the first organized golf club, but it's the St. Andrews Society of Golfers— formed ten years after and later renamed The Royal and Ancient Golf Club of St. Andrews—that was the game's birthplace. It was at St. Andrews that the first set of official rules was drafted; that it was determined a course should contain 18 holes. Golf, instead of existing only as an activity, was becoming an organized sport.

What did it all mean? Something simple, really. Golf clubs gave people places to play. Unlike most American country clubs of today, Scotland's courses were built for all of the local townspeople. Clubs were there for them, regardless of who they were, or how successful. Blessedly, golf in Scotland is just as accessible today.

Most clubs had courses that were situated on the rocky coastline, known as linksland, because it "linked" the land to the sea. Golf had originally been an inland game, but had grown so popular by the sixteenth century that Scotland's King James II had it outlawed for fear that it was cutting into his countrymen's vital archery practice. Not to be deterred, the golfers snuck away to remote seaside pastures to play, and when the ban was lifted nearly one hundred years later (gunpowder had arrived), the linksland courses had taken root and no one felt a need to return inland. In the late eighteenth century, organized golf clubs began forming in the seaside towns of Scotland. Not surprisingly, the trend spread to the seaside towns of England and Ireland, too.

What made this rapid development important back then is sociological in nature, and it's same reason that golf is important today. Often these seaside courses were situated as their towns' centerpieces, and were the logical place for townspeople to gather after the day's work was done, or during the weekend. It was clear from the beginning that golf's purpose was far more than advancing a small ball across a piece of land. Equally as important was the interaction it allowed people, not only with each other, but with nature as well. This can be the only explanation for golf's wild popularity. A day at the links with fellow townsfolk, the wind whipping, the waves of the mother sea crashing against the rocky shore . . . the Scots must have felt no closer to God anywhere but in a church!

This may seem a far cry from the posh country clubs of today's America, and in some ways it is. From the moment golf arrived in America in the late nineteenth century, it was a game played for the most part by the wealthy; few small towns built themselves around a fine golf course here, as they did in Europe. Why? Believe it or not, the American Revolution is at least partly to blame. Indeed, if America had had a king, golf in the United States would likely be much different today. His Majesty's subjects, as in Scotland, would have set up the first golf courses on open plots of his land, and anyone who wished to live near the course would have essentially paid rent to the King, attracting the middle class. However, since America is a democracy, and the land belongs to private citizens, the logical place to build golf courses has always been on the property of the men who owned the most land. These landowners were to become America's aristocracy, and when they climbed up the social ladder they took the game of golf with them. As a result, a quick glance at America's first golf clubs reveals a Who's Who list of historic and wealthy communities: St. Andrews, in Hastings on the Hudson, New York; Newport Country Club, in Newport, Rhode Island; The Country Club, in Brookline, Massachusetts; Shinnecock Hills Golf Club, in Southampton, New York; and Chicago Golf Club, in the posh Chicago suburb of Wheaton. These were the five charter members of the United States Golf Association, which was formed in 1894 to create standardized rules for the game and administer competitions.

Yet, regardless of the venue, golf remains at its core a game for all people, and its purpose is no different today than it was three hundred years ago. It endures and in no small way flourishes because it's a game that brings people and nature together, whether on the rocky coastline of Scotland, amid the sandy Pine Barrens in New Jersey, or across the vast desert in Arizona.

The game reveals itself to you slowly: There are always new things to discover, and new lessons to be learned, every single time you tee up the ball. Much of the reason the game is such a joy—and to be sure, so addictive—is that that freshness is always there; every round is in some way new. But the relationship of golf to nature is always present, and the first and undoubtedly most important lesson to learn. Simply put: Be sure to breathe the fresh air when you're out on the course. Smell the flowers, look at the trees, and listen to the birds sing—or, if you're in the right place, catch the waves washing up on shore.

Because for you, just as for our friends from St. Andrews and everywhere else, this is half the reason you're out there.

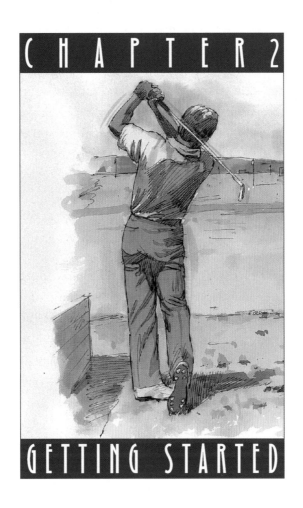

CHAPTER 2

GETTING STARTED

Making the decision that golf is a game you want to play is not all that monumental. Carrying it out, however, can seem a complex and overwhelming process, especially to the beginning golfer.

You can't walk into your local pro shop and announce that you're ready to play without a few prerequisite nuggets of knowledge and know how. Although it isn't all that complicated, the golf course does have its own modus operandi that's essential to everything running smoothly. By being truly ready to play, you can avoid embarrassing situations and ensure that your first trip to the golf course is a pleasurable one. Consider this chapter, then, a road map.

THE SPEED ISSUE

Hitting a golf ball is by no means an easy task for the unpracticed, and negotiating your way through a round of golf can be nearly impossible without a certain command of the swing. In most other sports, you can learn and improve through painful failure (after all, nobody cares if you roll gutterball after gutterball when you're learning to bowl), but what you do on the golf course affects all the players around you. If you're stuck in the fairway batting the ball around, the players behind you are forced to wait until you advance it out of their range. Thus, before you hit the golf course for the first time, it's important that you're sure of your ability to keep pace so your playing partners and the players behind you don't suffer.

So the thing to do is go to your local driving range. Bring a few clubs, or rent them there, and hit a bucket of balls. At the range you can make all the mistakes you want and nobody will care but you. It's not real golf, but it's fun, so indulge in it. The range will give you a chance to get used to the golf swing, making you a better player when you get to the course. The purpose of this initial visit, though, is to make sure your ball striking ability is at a level that will let you move around the course smoothly. If you're having trouble making contact or getting the ball in the air, you're not ready. Keep practicing or sign up for a few lessons with the local teaching professional

The driving range.

(see Chapter 8). Don't be discouraged. A little stick-to-itiveness goes a long way when you're learning the game. With a little diligence, you'll be getting the results you need in no time.

Your responsibility to the pace of play doesn't end with your ability to hit the ball, however. It only starts there. You'll find that if you make an effort to be speedy when you're on the course, other golfers will appreciate it and enjoy playing with you. Be ready to play when your ball is the farthest from the hole in your group, and don't dilly-dally between shots.

TEE TIME

The popularity of golf means it's a game that requires planning. Very rarely can you decide on a whim one Saturday afternoon that you'd like to play golf at the local public course—and find that it has space for you. At most courses, a reservation, or *tee time,* is required to secure a playing spot, and you must make this reservation anywhere from a day to a week in advance. Do yourself a favor: Call the courses in your area and find out their respective tee-time policies. These can vary from course to course, so it's a good idea to know whether your weekend round is going to require a week's worth of planning, or a day's.

TWOSOMES

You and a friend want to play. Fine. You should be aware, however, that some golf courses do not accept tee-time reservations for twosomes. Why? Financial considerations. Suppose a course has sixty tee times to fill during the day. It will do everything it can to make sure each of those sixty slots is filled with the maximum number of golfers allowed in a group, which is accepted as four (more than four makes for slow, plodding play). Giving a slot to a twosome instead of a foursome means losing revenue, so unless it can pair you up with another twosome, a course may refuse to give you an available tee time. Your options? In lieu of adding other regular players to your golf group, your best bet is to plan ahead. Courses often have twosome waiting lists, and the sooner you get you and your partner's name on one, the sooner you can be paired up with another twosome and penciled in on the tee-time sheet. Call a few days in advance and see what your course's policy is.

SINGLE GOLFERS

If you don't have a partner and you're not particular about who you play with, the process of securing a tee time for yourself changes. You win a little, you lose a little. On the one hand, you'll be hard pressed to find a course that will accept a tee-time reservation from a single golfer; on the other hand, you can usually play without advance planning. At most courses, you can simply call on the day you wish to play; the course will let you know if it can fit you in with a twosome or threesome that has a tee time. You'll be at the mercy of the day's schedule, but usually, if you want to play, you'll find a place.

EQUIPMENT

Buying golf clubs is a complex, not to mention costly, process (see Chapter 4), so don't run out and buy a set as soon as the impulse to play hits you. You do need something to play with, however, and most pro shops have rental sets available. (Call beforehand to make sure.) Don't expect a gleaming set of the latest model on the market. Although there are exceptions, rental sets are usually beat-up, outdated clubs that were donated to the shop for this

ONE SET PER GOLFER

Your friend has clubs and wants to introduce you to the game, so he offers to let you share his set for your inaugural round. Nice gesture, but most golf courses won't allow this. Passing clubs back and forth takes time and slows down the pace of play for the entire course. Be prepared for the rule that every golfer must have his or her own bag and clubs. If you can find an extra bag, you can ostensibly split a set in two and play that way, but you'll have to share a number of clubs, most frequently the putter, which slows down the play and makes things awkward for you and anyone else playing with you. So if you can't find a set, rent from the pro shop. You too will find the round more enjoyable if you're self reliant.

purpose. They still work, though, and while they might not look great they'll suit your needs just fine.

Balls, on the other hand, cannot be rented. You can buy them at your local sporting goods store or a golf discount house, or directly from the pro shop itself. In any case, buy more than you think you need, and put them in your bag when you play. I recommend two dozen. Golf balls travel hundreds of yards in the air when you hit them, and until you get accustomed to watching this phenomenon, it's easy to lose track of where they're flying. Add thick rough grass, trees, and water hazards, and your ball supply can dwindle before you know it. One of the most embarrassing—and most common—experiences of the beginning golfer is running out of balls toward the end of a round, and having to either borrow from someone else or just quit right there. Two dozen balls, though, should give you a cushion. And as you continue to play over the weeks and months, be careful to keep your supply at that two-dozen level. You never know when you'll run into a hole with a particularly ravenous water hazard or group of trees and expernience a golf ball "disaster." Eventually you'll find yourself playing not to lose balls, which will make you a better player. (See Chapter 4 for information on which balls to buy.)

DRESS CODE

Considering some of the golf fashions we've been forced to endure over the last few years, the notion that there's an unwritten dress code in the game is perhaps a frightening one. It does, however, exist. I make the point not to tell you what you should or shouldn't wear when you play, but to warn you of the general policies so you never have to deal with being turned away at a course.

Basically there are three levels of dress code. Level one is the no tank tops, no cut off shorts policy. It's pretty self explanatory and in effect at just about every course. Level two—prevalent at resorts and some public courses—forbids jeans and collarless shirts. Level three is reserved for the most exclusive private clubs. It disallows any shorts other than long bermudas and may even outlaw anything other than slacks altogether.

So here's your strategy: No matter where you play, leave the tanks and cut-offs at home. If it's too warm for pants, call the pro shop and ask if shorts are permitted. The chance that they're not is very slim. And invest in a couple of knit collared shirts if you don't already have them. Aside from preventing a hassle, the collared shirts will keep your neck from getting sunburned.

Golf shoes, incidentally, are optional just about everywhere, so don't invest until you're ready. Unless the course is wet, tennis shoes will suit you just fine. Avoid wearing dress shoes on the course; their slick soles can cause you to lose your balance.

GETTING AROUND THE COURSE

Let the record reflect that this section begins by stating that golf is a game made to be played on foot. That said, you generally have three options for getting around the course when you play: You can walk and carry your bag; walk and tow along your bag in a pull-cart; or put your bag in a gas or electric cart and ride. Pull-carts cost at most a couple of dollars in addition to the green fee, while gas or electric carts are usually at least $20 more. Which mode of transportation you choose usually depends on two factors—what kind of bag you have and what the golf course's policies are. If you have one of those big, heavy leather bags, you're not going to want to carry it. A pull-cart or electric cart is the way to go. Sometimes, too, your decision is made for you, because a number of courses—mostly at resorts

—require you to use an electric cart. The idea is that golfers play faster when they ride (debatable, incidentally), so if everybody rides the courses can get more players around in a day and collect more revenue. Again, if you have a preference one way or another, it's a good idea to check out its permissibility via the phone before you go to the course.

CHAPTER 3

THE GOLF COURSE

Even if you've seen golf on TV, the first time you step on a real golf course you may feel you've landed on an alien planet. There's grass everywhere. In some places there's water. Others there's lots of sand. Some grass is longer than other grass, and a different color. There are various objects stuck in the grass that mean various things. It's a mystery world to the newcomer. This chapter will give you a guided tour.

Okay. You've paid your greens fee, you've got your clubs, it's time to play. You head to the first tee. The *teeing ground,* or *tee box,* as it's sometimes called, is where you begin each hole, of which there are 18. At most courses, the teeing ground is a distinct area marked by shorter grass and objects—usually big

Hole
information
sign

Tee markers

Tee box

Ball washer

The teeing ground.

colored balls—called tee-markers. *Tee-markers* tell you where you should put your ball to begin the hole, and they're usually color coded based on ability. Blue-colored markers may be the first you see; they're farthest from the hole and therefore reserved for the better players. Red-colored markers are often the closest to the hole and usually called ladies' tees, but should be considered genderless. They're the suggested starting point for weaker players or beginners. White-colored markers are usually in the middle; they're for average players. Not all tee-markers are red, white, or blue, and not all courses have three of them. But the basic idea is that the farther a marker is from the hole, the better you have to be to play it. There are no rules determining who plays what, so use your best judgment.

Each hole is assigned two numbers: the *hole number,* 1 through 18, which indicates the sequence in which it should be played; and the *par,* usually 3, 4, or 5, which refers to how many strokes it should take a pro to hit the ball from the teeing ground into the hole. A hole's par is based, for the most part, on its length. If the *green* (the area containing the actual hole) is close enough to the teeing ground that you should be able to reach it in one shot, the hole is assigned par 3, allowing for two putts once on the green. If two shots are required to reach the green from the teeing area, the hole is assigned par 4, and if three shots is required, the par is 5. On most courses, the pars of all 18 holes add up to somewhere between 70 and 72, and that number is known as—this may sound familiar—*par for the course.*

Once you've selected the markers you're going to play from, stick a tee in the ground between the markers—being sure it's not in front of them—put your ball on the tee, and choose a club. On par 4s and 5s that club will generally be the driver, which is designed to hit off a tee. On par 3s, your choice will be whatever club you think will hit the ball the proper dis-

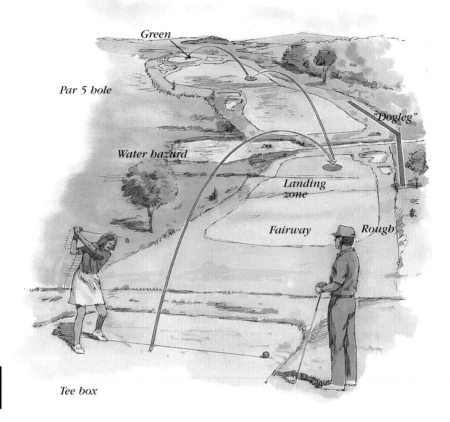

Par 5 hole

Green

"Dogleg"

Water hazard

Landing
zone

Fairway   Rough

Tee box

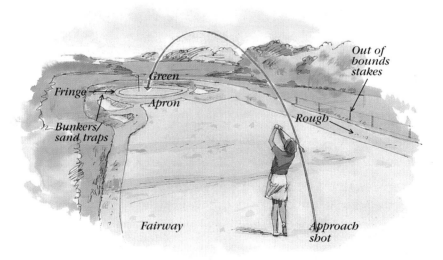

Out of
bounds
stakes

Green

Fringe

Apron

Rough

Bunkers/
sand traps

Fairway   Approach
shot

The parts of a golf hole.

tance—so that it stops on the green. Since par 3s can range anywhere from about 90 to over 225 yards in length, your club choice could be anything.

On par 3s, the object is for your tee shot to finish on the green, the area in the distance with defined, short grass and a flagstick in it. The *flagstick* marks where the hole is. On par 4s and 5s, the object is for your tee shot to finish in the *fairway,* which is the alley—as narrow as 25 yards or as wide as 100 —that runs most of the way from the tee to the green. The fairway has short grass, similar to Astroturf, that's easy to hit the ball from. Usually the fairway is surrounded by *rough,* which consists of longer grass that makes it more difficult for you to make clean contact with the ball. Avoid the rough.

Once you've hit your tee shot, the object of succeeding shots is to advance the ball from wherever it is (the fairway, hopefully) to the green. These shots toward the green are known as *approach shots.* As with a tee shot on a par 3, choose whatever club you feel will hit the ball the distance required for it to finish on the green. Since the flag marks the hole, you want the ball to finish as close to the flag as possible.

The green itself has the shortest grass on the course. It's like a carpet; the ball rolls across it easily. Surrounding the green is a slightly longer apron of grass called the *fringe,* and outside the fringe is usually rough. When your ball has reached the green, pull the flagstick out of the hole (putting with the flagstick in is illegal—more on this in Chapter 7) and lay it off to the side. Using your putter, try to roll the ball into the hole. Continue to putt until the ball goes in. Then count up how many shots it took you to move the ball from the tee to the hole; that's your score for the hole. Pick up your ball, put the flagstick back in the hole, and head for the next tee, where the process starts all over again. Eighteen holes, eighteen scores. Add up all the numbers and you have your score for the round.

HAZARDS

Just about any golf course you play will have *hazards,* stretches of no-man's-land that stand between you and the green. If your ball finds them, you will either be penalized or face a difficult escape shot. The most common hazards are *sand bunkers,* or *traps,* as they're less formally called. A sand bunker is a pit in the ground filled with sand. There's no penalty if your ball ends up in one, but, as you might imagine, it's more awkward to hit a ball while standing in sand that it is while on a nice secure patch of grass.

Also found on many courses are *water hazards,* often marked with red stakes. These can be creeks, streams, ponds, lakes, any sort of body of water. Stay away from the water. If your ball goes in, not only will it cost you a one-stroke penalty (adding an extra stroke to your score for the hole—see Chapter 7 on the rules), but you'll probably lose your ball.

Lastly, some courses have areas designated *out of bounds.* These areas, marked with white stakes, indicate places that the management does not want golfers hitting shots from—usually residences or heavily wooded areas. Hitting the ball out of bounds will cost you two strokes, and often a ball as well.

CHAPTER 4

EQUIPMENT

Woods, irons, putter, bag, balls, shoes, umbrella, clothes—there's a lot of stuff to be bought if you're going to play this game. And, as with golf itself, equipping yourself requires a precise strategy.

The wrong game plan will leave you with a closetful of unsuitable equipment and a severe dent in your checking account. Smart shoppers, on the other hand, will find equipment that truly fits not only their needs, but their budgets as well. A little knowledge and planning are all it takes.

A set of golf clubs is made up of four distinct club types: woods, irons, wedges, and a putter. They're different in many ways, although their basic construction is the same. All have a rubber grip for your hands; a shaft, usually made of steel or graphite; and a head, which makes contact with the ball.

WOODS: Woods are so named because for years they were made with wooden heads. Only in the last ten or fifteen years have metal-headed "woods" become the market staple, and because calling a club a "metal" is awkward (not to mention confusing, considering that it's different from an "iron"), the name *wood* has stuck. There are still wooden woods being made, but they're few and far between. The advantages of metal heads are many. Because they're cast from dies, it's much easier to manufacture them in mass quantities than it is woods, which are carved from blocks of persimmon or laminated maple. The casting process produces a hollow head that is perimeter weighted, making the club more forgiving of off center hits than wooden woods, which place most of their weight directly behind the sweet spot.

Woods have the longest shafts in the set, and because they create the most centrifugal force when swung, they hit the ball farther than other clubs. They also have their own subcategories: *drivers* (also known as 1-woods; they're the longest clubs in the bag, with the least loft, and are used to hit the ball off a tee); *fairway woods* (3-, 4-, and 5-woods, slightly shorter and more lofted than drivers, and used for long shots from the fairway and light rough); and *utility woods* (6-, 7-, 8-, and 9-woods, shorter and more lofted than the average fairway wood, and used for shorter shots from the fairway and long shots from deep rough and bad lies). The standard set of clubs has a driver and two or three fairway woods. Utility woods, while extremely valuable to many players, are usually optional.

IRONS: It's been a

hundred years since anybody made an iron that was actually made of iron, but, like woods, the name lingers on. (Traditions die hard in this game.) Irons are either forged from carbon steel or cast from stainless, and are shorter than woods. They're used for shots from the fairway and rough intended for the green;

WHAT DO THE NUMBERS MEAN?

Every golf club (with the exception of the putter) has a face angled upward to lift the ball into the air when struck. This angle is called loft, and the general rule of thumb is that the more loft *a club has, the shorter its shaft and the shorter the distance it will carry the ball. Lower-lofted clubs have longer shafts, which create more centrifugal force and, therefore, more powerful strokes. On the bottom, or sole, of most clubs a number is stamped, usually between 1 and 10, and very occasionally 11. This number refers to the club's loft. The lower the number, the less loft the club carries, the longer its shaft, and the longer the shot it will produce. So the longest-hitting club in the bag is usually a 1-wood, which carries the lowest loft—typically 10 degrees; and the longest shaft —usually forty-three inches. Working down through the set, the next club—in this case, a 2- wood—carries 4 degrees more loft in its face and has a shaft that's ¹/₂ inch shorter. This produces a slightly shorter shot that rises into the air more quickly. And so on down the line, until we get to the shortest, most-lofted club in the bag: the wedge, sometimes referred to as a 10- or 11-iron, which produces the shortest, quickest-rising shot of them all. As you might imagine, these shorter-shafted clubs are easier to control than the long ones.*

Clubs

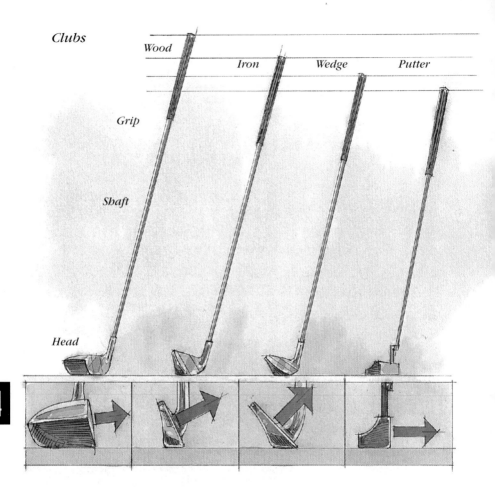

Wood

Iron   Wedge   Putter

Grip

Shaft

Head

Less loft usually means longer shots, except with the putter, which is used for the ball on the green.

CENTRIFUGAL FORCE

You certainly don't need to know physics to play golf, but you should have an idea of what centrifugal force is, because it's a major part of how golf clubs work and a phrase you may hear thrown around a lot during golf instruction. Literally, centrifugal means "fleeing center," and that's a good image to keep in mind when considering the concept.

If you tie a string to a rock, then twirl the string over your head like a lasso, centrifugal force will pull the rock outward, away from your hand, which is the center and stays relatively fixed. The only thing preventing the rock from truly "fleeing center" and flying away is the string. If you lengthen the string, the rock will fly around in a bigger circle at a faster speed. Golf clubs work the same way. Think of the clubhead as the rock, and the shaft and your arms as the string. Your body is the fixed center. The longer the string (in this case, the clubshaft), the larger the circle, and the faster the clubhead will move. The faster the clubhead moves, the farther the ball will fly when struck. Centrifugal force and, consequently, distance increase as the shaft of the club gets longer.

because their shafts are shorter than woods', they don't hit the ball as far and are easier to control. Irons have their own sub-categories, too: *long irons* (1-, 2-, 3-, 4-), *midirons* (5-, 6-, 7-), and *short irons* (8-, 9-). The standard set of irons carries 3- through 9-, with the 1- and 2-irons optional. However, it's increasingly common to see the 3- and 4-irons removed from the set in favor of higher-lofted fairway woods, such as the 5- and 7-woods, which are easier for the average player to hit.

WEDGES: Wedges look very much like irons, but because they're so specialized they deserve their own category. They're the shortest and most lofted clubs in the bag, which makes them useful around the green, where short, con-trolled shots, known as *chips* and *pitches,* are required. There are three different types: the *pitching wedge,* the least lofted of the three, used for short approach shots, chips, and pitches; the *sand wedge,* which has a special flange on its sole known as the *bounce* and is designed expressly for play from sand traps, but also useful from grass; and the *lob wedge,* the shortest and most-lofted club in the entire set, for high flying, soft-landing short shots around the

THE SAND WEDGE

There are two differences between a sand wedge and a pitching wedge. One is that the sand wedge usually has more loft—usually 50 degrees or more; the other is that it has more bounce.

Now, this doesn't mean the club will rebound off the ground when you drop it. Bounce *refers to a special flange on the sole of the club designed to make it easy to blast the ball out of the sand. On a regular pitching wedge, the trailing edge of the sole sits at the same level as the leading edge. On a sand wedge, the trailing edge sits lower than the leading edge. That means that the trailing edge hits the sand first, pre-venting the leading edge from digging and catching in it, and allowing the club to glide through it. This is vital to a good sand shot, and it" why you must have a sand wedge if you want to be at all suc-cessful at escaping from bunkers. (More on technique in the next chapter.)*

green. Most sets of irons include a pitching wedge, and occasionally a sand wedge. Don't let this fool you. The sand wedge, while optional in many sets, is one of the most important clubs in the bag. You must have one. Lob wedges, because they're the most specialized, are the rarest of the three clubs.

PUTTER: No club, however, is as specialized as the putter, which rounds out the set. A putter has little or no loft and is used for one thing only: to roll the ball on the green (and, hopefully, into the hole). Because putting is so different from the rest of the game, and because there are so few rules about what's right (good putting means getting the ball into the hole, not a particular style), putters are highly personalized. They're always sold separately from irons and woods.

THE SHAFT: No discussion of golf equipment would be complete without an extra nod to the clubshaft. Although the club manufacturers don't like to admit it (because so few of them make their own shafts), the shaft is the most important part of the golf club, and therefore worth knowing about.

Shafts are not all the same. Depending on construction and material, one shaft's properties can be much different than another's. The one property you should know about right away, however, is flex. When the club is swung the shaft flexes and then snaps back (if it didn't, it would be like hitting a shot with a telephone pole, and the ball would go nowhere), and some shafts flex more than others. The general rule is that the more a shaft flexes, the easier it is to swing, and thus the more suitable for the weaker or beginning player. Stiffer shafts, although they require more force, afford the golfer better control of the clubhead, and are therefore preferred by the stronger or better player. All shafts are marked with their level of flex. The standard references:

Woods

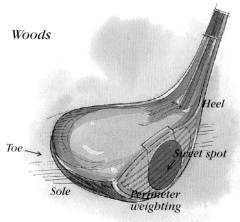

Heel

Toe →

Sweet spot

Sole

Perimeter
weighting

Iron

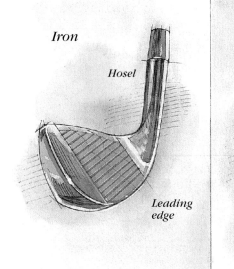

Hosel

Leading
edge

Putters

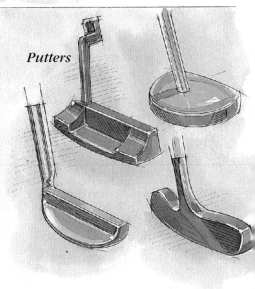

Wedges

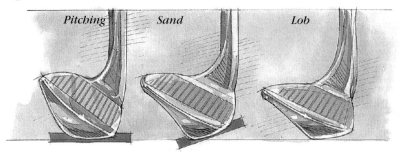

Pitching   Sand   Lob

Bounce

*The sand wedge's trailing edge hangs lower than the leading edge. This is
called bounce and distinguishes it from the pitching and lob wedges, which
have very little bounce.*

Flexible	Medium	Not Flexible
"A"	"R"	"S" or "X"
"soft"	"regular"	"firm"
"seniors"	"men's"	"tour"

Some manufacturers use numbers to indicate the flex of their shafts, which can be a bit confusing. Be sure to ask if you're not sure. Nothing can make a round of golf more frustrating than a shaft that's too stiff or too flexible for your swing. You do everything and yet the club won't perform, because it won't flex and snap back at the right moment for your swing speed.

SET OF YOUR OWN

The first few times you play, it's perfectly all right to rent clubs or borrow some from a friend. Once you've decided to really play the game, however, you're going to need a set of clubs that are really yours.

Don't be fooled by your local sporting goods store's golf department: Buying golf clubs is a lot like buying a suit. You can't make a smart purchase without trying them on first, and even then, you need a knowledgeable salesperson to help make sure they're tailored to your specific needs. And don't think that perfect fit isn't important. There are a lot of different clubs on the market, manufactured for many different levels of play. The wrong set will not only make it tough for you to play but retard your improvement process as well, ultimately making the game less enjoyable.

So avoid the impulse buy. Don't rush out and grab the shiny new clubs that all your golf-playing friends are talking about if you're just starting the game. And another thing: As much as you like your friends and respect their knowledge of the game, don't make any purchases based on their recommendations, unless your friends happen to be golf professionals. When you've decided that it's time for you to have a set of your own, don't go to the big discount house or the sporting goods store. Go to the pro shop at your local golf course. Ask to speak with the head professional. Tell him or her that you're just starting the game and you'd like to buy a set of golf clubs that will suit your needs. The golf professional is trained to match you up with a set of clubs that will work for you. Take advantage of this. Bring any questions and concerns you have to him. Here's a list you can arm yourself with to ensure you make the smartest buy:

Can I try before I buy? This is crucial; buying clubs without hitting them first is like buying a car without a test drive. And it doesn't matter if all your friends rave about a certain club; what works for one person may not work for the next, so never assume. When you test clubs, look for the set that feels the most comfortable in your hands and is easiest to swing without feeling flimsy.

Will the golf professional watch me test the clubs? Ideally, the pro will accompany you to the driving range while you test the clubs you're interested in. This will tell him what type of clubhead and shaft you need, as well as what set makeup (combination of woods and irons) best fits your game. Ask; you'll get everything from refusals to in-depth clubfitting sessions at no charge. Encourage the latter.

Which club feels the most comfortable? Perhaps the most important factor in your decision to buy. Once you tell the golf professional that you're a beginning golfer and looking to buy, he's going to suggest a number of different sets, all of which have the basic specifications (perimeter-weighted head designed for forgiveness and lightweight, more flexible shaft) suitable for a player of your ability. All of them will perform. Comfort will perhaps dictate which performs best for you.

Why this set of clubs? It's important to find out why your golf professional recommends one set of clubs over another.

Not only will this make you a more educated consumer, it will ensure that he's serving your needs, rather than his own. Most golf professionals are loyal and dedicated to their customers, but selling clubs is a business like anything else. Be alert.

 ## BAGS

Bags come in all shapes and sizes, from little canvas carryalls, designed to hold clubs and a few balls, to big leather staff bags, which hold everything you could possibly need on the golf course under any circumstance. They're enormous. Unless you have somebody to carry your bag from your home to your car and from your car to a cart at the golf course, don't bother with a staff bag. You will, however, need something larger than the aforementioned canvas carryall. In addition to storing a healthy supply of balls and tees, your bag should have room for an umbrella, an extra sweater, and rain gear, as well as sunscreen and a midround snack. It should also be sturdy enough to be strapped to a cart if necessary. Your best bet, then, is a light-weight, noncollapsible nylon bag with three or more pockets and a padded strap. These bags are popular for their versatility: They're light enough to carry, big enough to hold the needed supplies, and sturdy enough to take a bit of a beating. They're perfect for the golfer just getting into the game, because they'll serve you for years.

If they weren't included with your woods, check to see if the bag you choose comes with *head covers* (the puffy socks that cover woodheads). If it doesn't, buy a set. Head covers go a long way toward preserving the newness of your woods.

 ## BALLS

There are far too many variations of balls on the market for me to recommend a certain type, much less brand, to the beginning golfer. The only definitive advice you should take with you on your way to buy balls is to stay away from those that don't advertise a cutproof cover. Better players seeking a more delicate feel prefer balls with soft covers that will scuff and cut when mis-hit. The beginner can't afford this. Choose a ball that's willing to rough it and come back for more. Ask the pro or salesperson if the balls aren't clearly marked. Another bit of advice: Don't pay retail at your local pro shop. You'll get a much better price at a discount house or sporting goods store, and, since you can't test balls before you buy, you don't need the help of a golf professional anyway. Experiment with different balls. As you continue to play, you'll find a favorite that meets your needs.

COMPRESSION

As a general rule, balls come in three different compressions: 80, 90, or 100. Compression refers to the force it takes to compress the ball to its limit when struck. The lower the compression, the easier it is to "squeeze" the ball. Eighty-compression balls are usually marketed at women or seniors, 90-compression at "average" men, and 100-compression at hard swingers. Experiment with all the compressions if you wish. Chances are you'll notice a slight difference in feel, and perhaps a slighter difference in performance. Ultimately, the choice is yours. Play whichever you like best.

SHOES

If you really think about it, you don't *need* golf shoes to play golf. In most cases, tennis shoes provide a less complicated (and more comfortable) alternative. Golf shoes only become a necessity in wet weather, because the spiked soles will keep your feet anchored in wet grass where the flat soles of sneakers won't.

All debates aside, however, golf shoes are a major part of all that "stuff" you get when you decide to play the game, so chances are you're going to want them. There are a few things you should look for:

Comfort— Your first priority. Whether you walk or ride, if you don't have the right shoes blisters will happen. Don't put yourself through the hassle. Physical pain is not something you want to associate with learning golf. For years, there was no such thing as a comfortable golf shoe without a few weeks of breaking in. But when athletic-shoe companies like Nike and Reebok entered the golf market, a new concept was born: golf shoes as comfortable as sneakers. No one has figured out yet how to make classically styled wing tips feel like running shoes, but today virtually every manufacturer does offer a number of shoes that don't require any breaking in. Take advantage of the technology; your feet will be glad you did. Look for plenty of

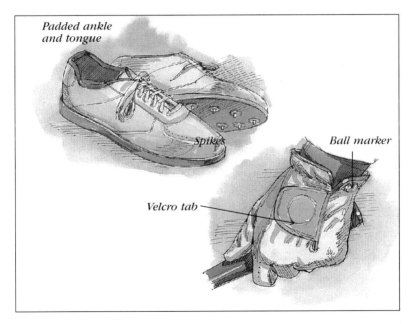

Padded ankle and tongue

Spikes

Ball marker

Velcro tab

Comfort and a snug fit are a priority in choosing a golf glove and golf shoes.

padding around the ankle and tongue, and go for a rubber or vinyl sole rather than a leather, which takes time to break in.

Waterproof—It doesn't have to rain for your shoes to run into water on the golf course. Between water hazards, surprise attacks by the sprinkler system, and morning dew, there are plenty of opportunities for your feet to get wet on a sunny day. Many shoes claim water resistance; go for the waterproof kind. A piece of canvas is water resistant; wrap your foot in it and step in a puddle and your foot gets soaked. Golf shoes are heavier than regular shoes as it is; a waterlogged pair can really make a round unpleasant. This means you're going to have steer away from the top of the line, finely crafted leather shoes. If that's a sacrifice you're not willing to make, consider that playing in expensive leather golf shoes is like trudging around in grass, dirt, and sand in dress shoes. They take a beating. Maintaining their looks and feel requires a lot of upkeep: waterproofing spray and weekly cleaning-and-polishing sessions. If you're willing to do this, go for the top-shelf shoes. But know that you can get shoes that look almost as good but require much less maintenance for less money.

Light Weight—If you plan on walking your way through a round—and you should—a relatively light shoe weight should be high on your priority list. The first thing you should do is check the sole construction of whatever shoe you're considering. Leather soled shoes will be considerably heavier than rubber- or vinyl-soled ones. Also, check the spikes themselves. For years, all shoes had steel spikes screwed into the sole. These are heavy. Today, most manufacturers offer shoes with highly durable plastic spikes that either screw into or are directly molded into the sole, which are much lighter.

GLOVES

Whether you play regularly or just visit the driving range once in a while, a golf glove is a worthy investment. Even if you work with your hands, the rubber grips on golf clubs are abrasive enough to cause blisters the first few times you play. A golf glove will prevent this. It goes on the left hand for a right-handed golfer and the right hand for a lefty, because that's the hand that has the most contact with the club. Gloves are available at your local pro shop, and should fit snugly, like a second skin. Buy one. Not only will it prevent blisters—which can end a round before it's really over—but, on hot days, it will give you a solid hold on the club even if your hands sweat.

There's actually a good reason why golf clothing was made chiefly of polyester for so many years. The fabric may not be all that attractive, or feel very good to the touch, but it does stretch. And in golf, that's a big plus. With all the twisting and turning involved in each swing, you don't want to wear anything that restricts your movement. Those beltless slacks and floppy collared shirts that gave golf a bad reputation also enabled golfers to wear somewhat formfitting clothes and still make uninhibited swings.

This is not to say you need to go to a seventies vintage store to get your golf shirts. These days, manufacturers have found a way to make their clothes mostly of cotton but still stretch slightly. What this means is that when it comes to shirts to play golf in, it's not a bad idea to choose a shirt designed for that purpose. And the styles aren't bad. The big floppy collars are gone in favor of smaller, knit ones. The colors won't blind you. And plenty of shirts are available in 100 percent cotton. They're a little oversized to make sure you can tuck in the tails and still have plenty of room to swing. Pants, incidentally, won't make much of a difference to your game; wear whatever you like within the dress code of the course you play.

Finally, wear a hat. Any hat. A round of golf is a four to five-hour event in the sun. Protect yourself as much as you can.

CHAPTER 5

BASIC TECHNIQUE

The best way to get started playing golf is to book a series of lessons with your local PGA professional to give yourself a solid grounding in the fundamentals. However, it's unrealistic to expect the

Checkpoints for a good grip: Start by setting the club face perpendicular to the target line. Hold the club under the heel of your left hand, keep it in the fingertips of the right, and make sure the v's formed by the thumb and forefingers of both hands point somewhere between your chin and right shoulder.

first-timer to dive so squarely into the deep end, and there's perhaps something to be said for discovering some things for yourself. In this spirit, what follows is a basic foundation of golf technique designed to prepare you for the shots you'll face in a typical round of golf.

THE GRIP

Simply put, the grip is the most important part of the golf swing. This may surprise you; after all, in baseball you just wrap your hands around the bat and swing away. But on the diamond you can hit the ball almost anywhere; on the golf course you have to hit the ball straight. Since your hands are your only connection to the club, a proper grip is essential.

A good grip is one that gives you a solid hold on the club without creating tension in your wrists, which must cock and uncock during the swing. If you experiment with a club in your hand, you'll find that holding it in your palms immobilizes your wrists. For this reason, the club is held primarily with your fingers, freeing up the wrists for their necessary movement. Here's a step-by-step procedure to follow:

1. Start with the left hand if you're a right-hander. With the club sitting squarely on the ground, the leading edge of the clubface (the flat area of the clubhead designed for striking the ball) perpendicular to the target, your left hand should be placed on the club with your palm parallel to the leading edge. The grip runs from the third fleshy pad on your forefinger to the outside of your palm, just above the heel. From there, your hand closes around the club. Your left thumb extends down the shaft so it rests just right of center. As you look down at your hand, you should be able to see two to two-and-a-half knuckles, and the V formed by your thumb and forefinger should point at your right ear or slightly right of it. Pressure is applied with your last three fingers. The left hand is the foundation of the grip for right-handers. You should be able to lift the club and swing it one-handed without your grip slipping or twisting around. If you can control the club with your left hand only, you're off to a great start.

2. Just as the back of your left hand faces the target as you prepare to grip the club, so does the palm of your right. With your right hand open and resting flat against the grip below your left, wrap your middle two fingers around the grip so the ring finger of your right hand is snugly against the forefinger of your left.

3. The little finger of your right hand rests in the channel between the forefinger and middle finger of your left hand. This is called the *overlap*, or *Vardon grip*. A variation on this, called the *interlock*, links your left forefinger and right little finger. Start by overlapping. As you become a little more familiar with the game, you can experiment.

4. The forefinger of your right hand crooks around the shaft like a trigger finger, and your right thumb should rest to the left of the grip, not on top. Don't squeeze the club with your thumb and forefinger; let them rest. Pressure should be applied with the two middle fingers of your right hand. As with your left, the V formed by the thumb and forefinger of your right hand should point at your right ear.

The feeling you should have when you grip the club—and the reason you overlap your forefinger and little finger—is that your hands are operating as one unit. Achieving this balance is important enough that it's worthwhile to spend plenty of time rehearsing your grip. Keep a club handy around the house so you can practice whenever you have the time. Here's a checklist to review:

■ The back of your left hand and the palm of your right face the target.

■ Your grip runs from the third fleshy pad of your left hand to the outside of your palm.

■ You should see two to two-and-a-half knuckles of your left hand.

■ The little finger of your right hand rests in the channel between the forefinger and middle finger of your left.

■ The Vs of both hands point at your right ear or slightly outside it.

THE SETUP

You want to accomplish three things when you set up to the golf ball: put your body in a position that allows it to swing the club freely, position the ball in correct relation to your stance, and align yourself properly, which for most shots means with your feet, knees, hips, and shoulders parallel to the target line.

Body Position:

Feet—The most basic stance places your feet at shoulder width, toes turned slightly outward. With the longer clubs—woods and long irons—your foot position widens to just outside your shoulders, for stability.

Knees—Not too bent, but not straight either. Your knees should be slightly flexed to engage the muscles of your legs and stabilize the rest of your body.

Hips—This is a crucial point in your setup and one where a lot of mistakes can be made. In a proper stance, you bend forward from your hips while keeping your back straight, which means that your rear end must stick out. Avoid rounding your back or bending forward from your waist; either will ultimately restrict your body and cause discomfort.

Shoulders—Because your right hand is lower on the grip than your left, your right shoulder should be lower than your left when you address the ball.

The Set Up: For a good set up, bend slightly at the knees and hips, and let your arms hang naturally from your shoulders.

Alignment: Alignment starts with the clubface, which must be perpendicular to the target line. Then, set your feet, knees, hips, and shoulders parallel to the target line.

Arms—Your arms are an extension of the club, so they shouldn't be tense or constricted. Let them hang naturally from your shoulders with about five inches between your left hand and your body.

Head—"Keep your head down" is the old duffer's advice. Don't buy it. Keep your head fairly erect, as if your chin were resting on a shelf. This will keep your spine straight and give your shoulders room to turn.

Ball Position: To understand the importance of where the ball is in relation to your stance, picture the swing as a circle tilted on its side, with your body in the middle. The point where the club makes contact with the ball should be the lowest point of that circle. Put the ball in the wrong place and contact will be made when the club isn't at its low point, which can result in many different shots, but very few good ones.

The general rule is that the low point with every club is opposite the inside of your left armpit. The exceptions: Move the ball back an inch with the short irons, which require a slightly descending blow; and move the ball forward an inch with the driver, which has less loft, and requires a slightly upward blow to clip the ball off the tee.

Alignment: Unlike target-oriented sports, such as basketball or archery, which require you to align yourself with the ball and the target and fire away, golf mandates that you stand to the side of the ball and line yourself up. In comparison to shooting a free throw, swinging a golf club is a little awkward; it's much easier to make a mistake. Be meticulous about your alignment. The old saying goes that you can have the greatest swing in the world, but if you line up incorrectly you won't hit a good shot. True. Get a head start by getting your alignment right. The key is to learn how to do it right and then repeat it, and the easiest way to accomplish this is by adopting a routine.

1. Stand behind the ball so it's directly between you and the target. Then walk to the side of the ball and place the clubface behind it so the leading edge is perpendicular, or square, to the target line.

2. Take your grip, keeping the clubface square.

3. Place your feet so they're parallel to the target line and the ball is opposite the inside of your left armpit.

4. Swivel your head to look at the target, then back at the ball. You're ready to swing.

THE SWING

Once you've taken your grip and set up to the ball, the golf swing is made up of three parts: the *backswing*, in which the club is swung above your head; the *downswing*, when the club is swung down and contact with the ball is made; and the *follow-through*, which occurs after contact is made.

The Backswing: A good backswing accomplishes one thing: It puts you in position to make a good downswing. This means when you reach the top of your swing—your backswing is complete—you should be able to deliver the clubhead squarely down the target line to the ball without any compensations. A few keys to keep in mind to make sure this happens:

1. Start the backswing by dragging the club back along the target line with your arms straight. For the first eighteen inches, the arms and club should act as one unit. Keep your wrists and lower body quiet.

2. Your arms and shoulders control the backswing until the club reaches hip height. At this point, the shaft should be parallel to the ground and the target line, and the toe of the club should point straight up. Focus on keeping your weight centered on the inside of your right foot.

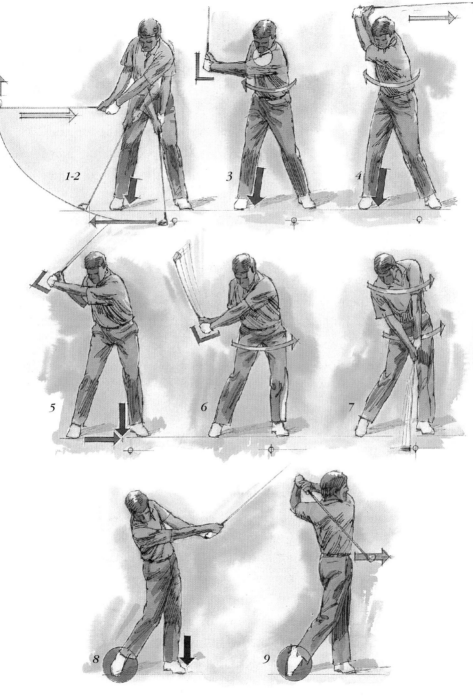

The swing.

3. Your right foot and flexed right knee become your anchor as you rotate your torso to complete the backswing. By the time your left arm is parallel to the ground, the club should be perpendicular and your left shoulder turned almost equal to your chin. The rotation of the left shoulder forces your hip, knee, and foot to turn in slightly, too.

4. The remainder of the backswing is accomplished by lifting the club to the top of the circle with your arms. At the top, the club should point at the target, your body should be fully coiled, and your weight should remain on the inside of your right foot.

The Downswing: In the downswing, everything happens in reverse order from the backswing: Instead of your arms starting the movement and pulling your shoulders, hips, knees, and feet after them, your feet start the downswing and pull your knees, hips, shoulders, arms, hands, and, finally, the club after. Picture the downswing starting from the ground up. Here's how it breaks down:

5. The first move of the downswing is the replanting of your left heel, or—if your heel has remained on the ground—the shifting of weight to your left foot. Avoid the impulse to start the downswing by pulling your arms down or unwinding your shoulders. This is how bad shots start.

6. As your left knee and hip rotate toward the target, your shoulders resist and stay coiled. Your arms do nothing but drop straight down, following gravity. As they do so, your wrists cock, creating what is known as the *delayed-hit position*.

7. Once your arms have dropped and your wrists are fully cocked, your shoulders may unwind freely through impact. Your arms will trail and your wrists uncock naturally. By the time impact is made, your hips and shoulders have rotated past the ball and the club is just starting to catch up.

The Follow-through: Even though you've already made contact and the ball is on its way by the time of your follow-through, it's no less important a part of your swing. Because the downswing happens so fast, focus instead on your follow-through when you wish to made adjustments: It reflects what happens in the rest of your swing. In short, a good follow-through indicates a good swing.

8. As the club comes through the point of impact and extends into the initial stage of the follow-through, your right arm straightens and your left begins to fold at the elbow—almost a mirror image of the backswing. By this point the majority of the weight has transferred to your left foot, and your right has begun to roll up onto its toe.

9. At the finish of the swing, your hips and shoulder have rotated so your belt buckle faces the target. Your folding left arm comes up and around your body, and your right arm comes across your chest. This is the natural result of a good downswing. Your weight rolls over to the outside of your left foot, and your right comes completely up onto its toe.

The swing may seem complicated, because everything from your head to your toes gets involved along the way. But don't be fooled; in no way are you expected to remember all or even part of what you've just read as you stand over the ball and prepare to swing. The last thing you want to do as you stand over the ball is run through a long mental checklist of things the various parts of your body should or shouldn't be doing. No golfer can process all that information. Instead, use the breakdown as a reference. Check your swing positions in the mirror against the pictures, or go back and reread the analysis occasionally to refresh your mind. It's important to know what happens during the golf swing—but this is not to say you should be thinking about it when you hit the ball.

When you're actually hitting the ball, you want to keep it as simple as possible. Most of the little intricacies in the breakdown will occur automatically if your preparation is good. Make sure you've aligned yourself correctly and taken the proper grip, then choose one thought to drive your swing. Here are some possibilities. Experiment until you find one that works for you, or discover one of your own.

- Swing the club straight back, and straight through.
- Turn your torso back, then turn it through.
- Coil your body like a spring, then release it.
- Imagine the swing as a circle tilted on its side, and trace that circle with the clubhead.

PITCHING AND CHIPPING

Not all shots in a round of golf are full swings. Often you'll be faced with a short shot to the green—anywhere from ten to sixty yards—that requires you to make a shorter swing to place the ball near the hole. These are called pitch shots and chip shots and, as you progress in the game, you'll quickly realize that your proficiency in them can make or break your score for the round. A good pitch or chip will make up for several mediocre full shots and turn what could easily have been a high score for a hole into a respectable one.

Pitch shots are like miniversions of full swings. Very little is different, except your hands rarely get higher than hip height on the backswing. Using a pitching wedge or sand wedge for loft, assume your normal grip or—if you wish—choke down an inch for an extra feeling of control. You'll need to make a slight adjustment in the setup. Rather than placing your feet at or just outside shoulder width, assume a narrower stance for a pitch

Pitch

Choke down on grip

Open stance

Pitch: The pitch shot requires a shorter version of the full swing: as you swing the club back and through, allow your wrists to hinge slightly and your weight to shift.

Chip

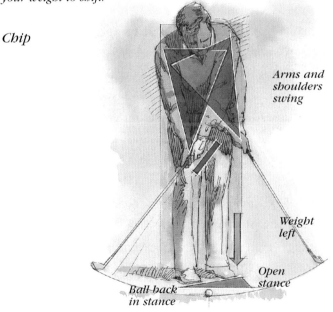

Arms and shoulders swing

Weight left

Open stance

Ball back in stance

Chip: The chip shot requires a longer version of the putting stroke: keep your wrists quiet and your body still as the arms and shoulders control the stroke.

shot, with your feet a few inches inside shoulder width. And instead of setting your feet square to the target, pull your left foot back a few inches, so that your feet point 30 or so degrees left of the target. This opens your body, giving you a better look at the target line and also making it easier for you to swing the club through. It will restrict your backswing slightly but, since you're only taking the club halfway back, you won't notice. Keep your grip pressure light and swing the club back slowly. Coming through, you should feel as if you're tossing a softball underhand with your right hand. Don't try to flip your wrists or lift the ball into the air. The loft on the club will send the ball airborne easily, producing a shot that will land softly on the green and roll almost as far as it flew.

Chip shots are smaller shots that fly only a short distance, then roll most of the way to the hole. They're used when the ball is just off the edge of the green and there's a small patch of grass that will prevent the ball from rolling straight onto the green. Chipping is similar to putting in that a very short stroke is used, controlled primarily by your arms and shoulders with virtually no movement in the hands and wrists. With the same open stance used for the pitch shot, play the ball an inch or two farther back, toward your right foot, and shift most of your weight to your left foot to ensure that you make a descending blow on the ball and don't hit the ground first. Using anything from a 5-iron, for longer shots requiring a lot of roll, to a sand wedge, for short little "pops" that travel only a few feet in total, choke down a few inches on the grip. Then, by rocking your shoulders back and through, hit the ball. You don't need to make big swing—eighteen inches back and through is plenty, for the club will do all the work when it comes to loft and distance. The object of the chip shot is to get the ball over whatever is between you and the green and get it rolling as quickly as possible. The more a shot rolls, the more control you'll have. Keep this in mind.

Elements of a solid putting stroke: Palms face each other, eyes over the ball, arms and shoulders swing the club back and through like a pendulum.

PUTTING

If you've ever watched golf on TV, you may have found it difficult to distinguish one pro's swing from another's, because they all share a number of fundamentals. Putting is a different story. Putting strokes are almost like snowflakes—no two are exactly alike—because in truth, there is only one rule of putting technique: Do whatever works. That's why you'll see some pros crouched over when they putt and some standing tall; some with wide stances and some with their feet together; and a multitude of different grips and strokes: short pop strokes, long wristy strokes, even strokes that impart sidespin. With the amount of money pros play for, they don't care what their putting strokes look like as long as the ball goes in. Chances are you won't play for that kind of money, but since putting makes up 50 percent of each round's strokes, you'll soon realize that adopting this whatever-it-takes attitude makes good sense. However, everybody needs a starting point. Consider the following, then, not a list of the "fundamentals," but a description of the simplest way to learn to putt. Remember: Whatever it takes:

1. Start with the grip. The simplest way to putt is to control the stroke with your arms and shoulders with no assistance from the hands or wrists, so the standard putting grip is designed to immobilize them. Instead of holding the club in your fingers as you would for a full shot, hold a putter in the palms of your hands; this effectively keeps your wrists locked. First, take the club in your right hand only, about four inches from the top of the grip. There's a flat ridge on the front of the grip; rest your right thumb on this flat ridge, keeping your palm parallel to the clubface. Now add your left hand. The thumb rests on top of the flat ridge and tucks under the pad of your right hand. The left forefinger overlaps the ridge between your right little finger and forefinger, and the last three fingers of the left hand wrap around the end of the grip, tucking under your right hand slightly. The end of the grip should lie in the groove formed by the two pads at the heel of your left hand.

2. Again, there are no rules for the setup, although you'll probably be most comfortable—at least initially—with a stable, shoulder-width stance, a slight flex in your knees, and a forward bend from your hips. However, what you may find most helpful is the position of your head. By positioning your head so your eyes are directly over the ball, you'll have the best view of the line of the putt. This is the easiest way to ensure that you are aligned correctly and making a straight-back, straight-through stroke.

3. To make the actual stroke, imagine that a triangle is formed by your hands, shoulders, and arms, and that it's hanging from the bottom of your neck. Then swing that triangle back and through like a pendulum. Your wrists stay quiet, and the club merely follows along.

SAND PLAY

Nothing strikes more fear into the average amateur than watching his or her ball roll into a greenside bunker. All it takes is one bad experience in the sand to make it a golfer's least favorite place. Ironically, though, the average bunker shot is among the easiest in golf—if you know the proper technique. Few amateurs do, however. You can get a big head start on the game by familiarizing yourself with how a sand shot works. It doesn't take a lot of talent, just understanding.

What makes a sand shot unique is that it's the only shot in golf where the club doesn't make contact with the ball. Remembering this is important, because if you step into a bunker and try to pick or lift the ball out with a club, you'll rarely be successful. Instead, the club hits the sand behind the ball and the sand pushes the ball out and up into the air. In effect, the club cuts a layer of sand out of the bunker and the ball flies out with it. Here's the basic technique:

1. Set up with your feet at shoulder width and pointing about 30 degrees left of the target. Dig your feet into the sand to stabilize your footing as much as possible. You should feel as if the ball is opposite your front foot.

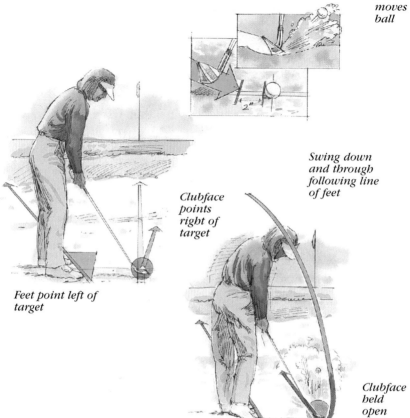

Sand moves ball

Swing down and through following line of feet

Clubface points right of target

Feet point left of target

Clubface held open

The sand explosion is the only shot where you deliberately miss the ball: hit the sand and it will force the ball up and out.

2. Being careful not to touch the clubhead on the surface of the sand (this is a penalty; see Chapter 7 on rules), take your normal grip, except rotate the club in your hands so that when you are relaxed the clubface points right of the target. Opening the face like this increases the loft of the club as well as the bounce (see sidebar, Chapter 4), ensuring that the club won't get stuck in the sand.

3. Make a long, slow swing along the line of your feet. The crucial thing to keep in mind here is that you must hit the sand before the ball, so aim for a spot about two inches behind.

Concentrate on keeping the clubface pointing to the sky through and past impact. The ball will float out on a layer of sand.

THE MIND GAME

If you haven't heard it yet, somebody will lay the old adage on you soon enough: Golf is 90 percent mental. Don't misconstrue this statement. It implies that good golf is achieved mostly through some elusive Zen mind control that propels your ball around the course. Not so. A solid grasp of the fundamentals of the long game, short game, and putting is the bedrock of good golf. That said, however, it must be acknowledged that golf is a game of strategy. It's a chess match, you against the golf course, and in order to be successful you must think your way through a round. This means being able to assess whatever obstacles the course throws at you during a round and make smart choices about how to deal with them. Wind, rough, hills, trees, what do you do? Basic technique isn't enough.

Smart choices, of course, come mostly from experience, but there are a few rules of thumb you can start with. Here then are some typical situations in which you might find yourself during the course of a round—and ways to handle them:

Wind in your face—A headwind will increase the backspin of a ball hit into it. The extra backspin will cause the ball to rise, and a ball rising into a headwind achieves less distance. To counter this and prevent the wind from controlling your ball, you must hit a shot that flies on a lower trajectory—underneath the wind. Start by dropping down two clubs from what you would ordinarily use. That is, if you are 150 yards away from the green, and if under still conditions you hit your 5-iron 150 yards, choose the 3-iron. Adjust your stance so the ball is back a little farther, about equidistant between your two feet. Then make a normal swing, with about 75 percent of your normal effort. Moving the ball back in your stance encourages a lower trajectory, and the less-lofted club and easier swing minimize backspin, producing a lower, more boring shot.

Wind at your back—Anytime your ball has the chance to ride the wind it will achieve more distance, so you'll need less club. Be aware, however, that a tailwind also reduces backspin, so the ball will roll more when it hits the ground. This is great for tee shots, but for shots to the green you won't be able to count on the ball stopping quickly as it does under normal conditions. If there isn't room for the ball to roll up to the pin, don't expect to hit it close.

Crosswinds—Winds from the side will blow your ball off-line, so compensate by adjusting your alignment in the direction the wind is coming from. That is, if the wind is blowing left to right, aim farther left so the wind will carry your ball back to your intended target.

Hilly lies—Rarely will you get a perfectly flat lie on the golf course, so you must be able to handle hilly lies. The key to all such shots is to adjust yourself to the hill—that is, to alter the way you stand to the ball so you can make as normal a swing as possible. Here's how:

ball above feet—This lie will make the ball want to fly left of the target, and the more lofted the club you use, the more this is true. (Set a club down on its heel with the toe in the air and you'll see how this works: The clubface will point left.) To counter this, aim right of your target and move the ball back an inch or so in our stance. Concentrate on swinging a bit more around your body, rather than on a vertical plane.

ball below feet—Conversely, shots will tend to fly right from this lie, because angling the club onto its toe points the clubface in that direction. Increase your knee flex so you're not reaching too far for the ball, aim left of your target, and move the ball an inch or so forward in your stance. You won't be as mobile or balanced, so don't swing too hard.

uphill lie—The hill will add loft to whatever club you're using, so prepare for a high trajectory shot. If the hill is extreme, you'll want to move up a club or two from your ordinary choice to get the distance you need. Focus on staying centered and balanced as you swing through the ball; the tendency is to fall back on the hill, which will send the ball left of your target.

downhill lie—The hill will decrease the loft of your chosen club, so expect a lower shot that may not stop so quickly when it hits the green. To make sure that you hit the ball before you hit the ground, you'll want to move the ball about an inch back in your stance, but beware: This lie encourages the ball to go to the right off the clubface, and the farther back you move it, the more pronounced this effect will be. Adjust yourself by aiming left of your target, and concentrate on not allowing the hill to pull you ahead of the ball as you swing down and through.

The rough—How well you can hit the ball out of the rough depends largely on how thick the rough is. If it's so thick that you have problems getting the club through the grass on a practice swing, abandon all ideas of hitting the ball at the green. Take out a wedge and slash the ball back into the fairway. From a less penal rough you can go for the green, but expect the ball to come out flying lower and with much less backspin. You'll get more roll but less carry, so consider moving up a club. Be warned, though: You'll have much more difficulty hitting long irons out of the rough than mid- and short irons and, for that matter, fairway woods. When faced with a long shot from the rough, a 5-wood or utility wood is a much better bet than a 3- or 4-iron. Stay away from the lower-lofted fairway woods, as well.

Tree trouble—You don't have to be a beginning golfer to hit the ball into the trees; it happens to all of us, and when it does, careful analysis of the situation is required. As with all so-called "trouble" shots, the question you must ask yourself is: Is going for the green worth the risk? The answer, of course, depends on the situation. If there's a narrow gap in the trees leading to the green that demands the best shot of your life to hit the ball through, it's not worth the risk. Chances are far greater that you'll miss the gap and hit another tree, and who knows where your ball will bounce. In this situation, take a short iron or wedge and chip the ball back into the fairway. If the gap is bigger, however, and you're confident you can get the ball through it, go for it, but pay attention to your lie. If the ball is sitting down in the rough or in a patch of leaves, odds are you won't make solid contact, which will reduce your chances of hitting a good shot. Consider all the pros and cons before trying a "hero" shot. Usually your best bet is just to take your medicine, chip the ball back into the fairway, and play from there.

Reading greens—Half the skill in putting is the ability to determine how the various slopes and grains of the grass are going to affect your shot. This is called *reading the green.* There's no secret; you do it by sight. Crouch down behind your ball so you're looking straight past it to the hole, and examine the way the green slopes. Sometimes there will be no slope at all; other times, multiple undulations. Of course, if your putt must slope uphill to the hole you'll need to hit it a little harder, and vice versa for downhill putts. Putts that slope left to right or right to left require a judgment call on your part as to how far outside the hole to aim. You'll get a feel for these putts as time goes by. In the early stages of your game it's just a matter of trial and error.

If you don't get a clear picture of how your putt will move, or *break,* when you crouch behind your ball, then go around to the other side of the hole, crouch, and look back at your ball. Between these two positions you should get a pretty good idea of the slope of the green. In the interest of speedy play, however, go behind the hole only as a last resort. Only the most confusing of putts will be unreadable from the behind the ball.

Another thing to keep in mind when you're putting is the grain, or direction in which the grass is growing. Even though the grass is only millimeters long, grain can make a difference in certain situations. Putts running with the grain will tend to be faster, requiring less force; putts running against the grain will be slower, requiring a harder hit. Grain, as a rule, runs in the direction that water would drain off a green. So if there's a pond in front of the green, you can count on the grain running toward the pond. Look also for hills around the green; grain tends to run downhill. Sometimes, however, grain will play a prominent part on a relatively flat green. In that case, it usually runs to the west, toward the setting sun.

BASIC TECHNIQUE

FIRST TEE

CHAPTER 6

PUBLIC, PRIVATE, AND RESORT COURSES

Not all golf courses are created equal. Most likely you'll begin your golfing life at a public course, where anybody is allowed to play, but as your game progresses you'll have the opportunity to tee

The Locker Room

up at private courses, where you must be a member or guest of a member to play, and resort courses, which are affiliated with hotels and often part of a lodging/golf package. The modus operandi at each of these three types of courses is different, so before you try to navigate through uncharted waters, familiarize yourself with each:

THE PUBLIC COURSE

Because they're open to anyone, most public courses get a lot of use. That means they're jam-packed on weekends, and often crowded during the week. Reserving a tee time is usually a must if you don't want to be stuck at the course for hours waiting to play. Be sure to check out a course's tee-time policy in

The Practice Green

advance: Some will allow you to reserve tee times a week in advance, others accept reservations only on the day you wish to play.

It's customary to arrive at the course at least forty-five minutes before your tee time to warm up, buy any items you may wish in the pro shop, and change your shoes, if you wear spikes on the course. (Don't drive in your golf shoes.) The longtime practice of public-course golfers is to change shoes in the parking lot and walk to the pro shop ready to play. This is the easiest way. Many courses have a clubhouse with a locker room, and if you plan on sticking around after your round and having a drink in the clubhouse, you may wish to bring a lock with you and change your shoes in the locker room. But if you plan on leaving right after your round, do what public-course golfers have been doing for decades and change your shoes on the back bumper of your car.

Once the shoe-changing issue is resolved, your first stop is the pro shop, to check in. You'll pay your greens fee there, plus any cart rental, and take care of whatever purchases you may need, such as balls, a glove, a hat, and so on. If the course has a driving range, do yourself the favor of buying a small bucket of balls and hitting a few easy shots on the range to warm up and establish a rhythm for yourself. The pro shop will sell you either the balls or a token that you insert into an automated dispenser. Your other warm-up option is a practice putting green. Most courses have them. Take a few minutes before your round to hit practice putts of various lengths, just to make putting a familiar activity before you get onto the course.

At one point or another, the people in the pro shop may tell you to see "The Starter." The starter is usually somewhere near the first tee, and is responsible for making sure that all the groups start smoothly and on time, so there are no undue delays. Often the pro shop will give you a receipt for your greens fee, which you present to the starter before you tee off,

The Starter

as you would a lift ticket in skiing. Hold onto your receipt, and be sure to keep track of time. Generally you should report to the first tee ten minutes before your tee time. If you're late, the starter may well give your time away, especially if the course is crowded.

Public courses can be municipally or privately owned. There's a difference. A privately owned public course is usually more concerned with the bottom line: In other words, the object of operating the course is to make money. This usually means that whatever money is put into upkeep (a massive investment) is kept at a level that allows the corporation to stay comfortably in the black. For this reason, you may find that some privately owned public golf courses are poorly maintained yet have higher greens fees than municipally owned. Municipally owned courses benefit from the fact that the local government is bound, at least to some degree, by the responsibility of providing a place for its residents to play golf. If the course is near a large city, expect it to be crowded, and the course conditions to show the wear and tear of heavy use. Public courses in more suburban or rural areas often get less use and can be in much better shape than the average city course. However, spotty conditions don't make the game any less enjoyable. In fact, public courses have a certain grassroots feeling to them that private and resort courses lack.

Much of this has to do with people. Unless you bring three friends with you, you can expect to be paired up with at least one complete stranger every time you play. That's what makes public-course golf so great: The cast of characters is usually pretty interesting. You'll meet all kinds of people, from beginners to seasoned hustlers not carved in the country-club mold. There's a laid back atmosphere but a true enthusiasm for the game, as well. Remember that in golf's birthplace, Scotland, the game is played more by the common man than anybody, and you'll understand the special charm that public courses hold.

Private clubs are a little like Ivy League schools. There's a lengthy application process, you usually have to know someone to get in, and, once you are accepted, it costs you a lot of money to stay there. Exclusivity is the name of the game, so unless you're well connected and totally committed to making the game a large part of your life, you don't have to worry about joining a private club right away. However, if you don't already know somebody who belongs to a private club, you'll meet one soon enough, and before you know it the opportunity will come for you to play at this club as his or her guest. Playing the course—usually a better-maintained and more challenging lay-out than your average public course—is a treat. But be aware that at many private clubs, especially the older ones, you'll have a few formalities to deal with along the way. Arming yourself with the knowledge of how things work will help you eliminate any awkward moments.

First of all, bring cash. You won't pay for your greens fee or cart, if you take one—they'll be charged to your host—but there are bag handlers and locker room attendants to be tipped, and, if you choose to take a caddie instead of a cart, you may have to pay him or her in cash. So make sure you're well stocked, just in case.

Most likely your car will be met by the bag handlers, who'll ask who you're playing with (answer: your host) then take your clubs and put them either on a cart or on a rack by the pro shop. For this you may give them a dollar tip. It's done custom-arily, if not out of sincere gratitude for the service, then out of respect for your host, who looks bad if you look bad.

One of the perks of belonging to a private club is that you get your own locker, so, since your host will be changing his shoes in the locker room, do the same. Chances are the locker room attendant will be expecting you and have an empty locker waiting, where you can store your street shoes and anything else you don't need for the round.

After your round is complete, the bag handlers will clean your clubs and either leave them by the bag drop in the parking lot or take them directly to your car. Again, no less than a dollar tip is customary. In the locker room, give your shoes to the locker room attendant; he or she will take a minute to clean off the dirt and grass and put a bit of polish on them. The standard tip for shining the shoes and setting you up with a locker is a few dollars.

If you're wondering what gives with all the pomp and circumstance, well, it's tradition, and that's the way private clubs are. But that's not why people spend tens and sometimes hundreds of thousands of dollars to be members. Generally, this is because of the golf courses. As a rule, private courses are the best maintained, with the best-designed layouts around, because they simply have more money to spend and fewer

The Bag Handler

Sometimes a caddie's knowledge of the course can be invaluable.

golfers to tear up the course. Of the five greatest courses in America, only one—Pebble Beach Golf Links—is open to the public. And it costs over $200 to play there. That's why, if you get a chance to play a private course, take it. Playing its lush fairways and unblemished greens will be worth the formalities.

CADDIES: Years ago, most courses, public and private, had caddies available for hire. Today, motorized carts have taken over at public courses and caddies are strictly a private-club phenomenon. Hiring one is recommended. Not only will a caddie allow you to walk the course without carrying your bag, but he or she may also serve as a navigator, coach, and second set of eyes to follow—and find—some of your errant shots.

Your host will inform the caddie master (similar to the starter at a public course) whether you'll take a cart or caddie. If you take a caddie, chances are he'll carry both bags, one on each shoulder. You can request a private caddie just for yourself, but there's a good chance you'll be refused or charged a double rate. A foursome usually gets two caddies; in the case of a threesome, the standard procedure is to take two caddies, one carrying double bags, one carrying single, who switch after nine holes.

Some caddies have a real insider's knowledge of the golf course and its nuances; others don't but like to make believe they do. This is also traditional. Use your best judgment. It won't take long before it's clear whether your caddie is truly on the money or not. If you happen to land a good one, take advantage of him. The game gets a lot easier, and even more enjoyable, if you can surrender yourself to a tour guide. Your improved play will show you the effect that good strategy and course management can have on your game.

If your caddie's advice isn't quite clicking, and it begins to become unwanted, don't let it bother you or complain to your host. Just say, "No advice, please. I'm fine on my own." This should be just fine with the caddie. His job is to serve you. If you don't want advice, he won't give it. You're paying the bill. Get what you want.

There are a few things you should expect from any caddie. Besides carrying your bag and being ready to give you a club when you need one, he should keep your clubs and ball clean, know how far away from the hole you are on every shot, and keep his eyes peeled so he has a beat on the ball every time you hit it.

THE SEMIPRIVATE COURSE

Occasionally you'll run across a course with this designation. Usually it means that the course is open to the public but has a membership roster. Often the members are residents of an affiliated housing community, and in return for their membership status they get reduced rates on greens fees and preferred tee times. In some cases, the course may be restricted to member-play-only on weekends but open to anyone the rest of the week. Call beforehand to get all the specifics.

Caddies are paid a by-the-bag rate. A typical caddie fee is $25 per bag for 18 holes, plus tip. Your host may choose to charge the caddie fees to his or her account, but you should always assume that you'll pay cash. The tip is up to you, but unless the caddie does a really horrible job—like perhaps losing a club—it's customary to give him somewhere around $10 for a $25 bag. Feel free to give more if he really did well by you.

THE RESORT COURSE

If you're on vacation and you've chosen to go where it's warm, there's a good chance a golf course is nearby. It's also likely that said course is linked in some way with a hotel or a number of hotels in the area. This is a resort golf course. You don't have to be a member to have playing privileges, but very often you must be staying at one of the affiliated hotels. How do you know? Ask at the front desk or concierge stand of your hotel. The staff will be able to do one of three things for you. Either (1) secure you a tee time at a local course, complete with an electric cart, and charge it to your master bill at a discounted rate; (2) reserve you a time and cart at a discounted rate, although you'll have to pay at the course; or (3) get you a tee time and cart but no discounts. If you're not staying at an affiliated hotel, you can usually still play at a resort course, but it will cost you extra. Call first and see if there are any times available.

Once you've secured a time for yourself, the drill is similar to that of a public course, with a few exceptions. First of all, when you arrive at a resort course, very often there will be bag handlers waiting for you. They'll help you get your clubs out of the car and immediately put them onto an electric cart. The majority of resort courses require that you take a cart; it's a revenue producer. If you want to walk, be sure to ask beforehand if it's allowed. If it isn't—and chances are it isn't—don't expend a lot of energy searching for a course that allows walkers. You'll be hard pressed to find one in vacation country.

Resort courses also invest more money into things like clubhouses and locker rooms than most public courses, so if you're going to change your shoes, eschew the parking lot for the more comfortable locker room. And no need to rush off after the round, either. You're on vacation. Stick around, enjoy yourself, have a beer and some peanuts. It's part of the experience.

Higher prices are part of the deal, too. You can expect the greens fees at a resort course to be at least twice that of the average public layout. Add the mandatory cart and maybe a few balls at inflated prices and the discount that being a hotel guest won you may seem more symbolic than anything else. However, there is a payoff. For the extra money you get better facilities. In addition to the setting usually being picturesque, the courses are better maintained, the carts in better condition, and the service better. Often there will be snack carts touring the course, selling food and beverages to golfers as they play. The bag handlers will not only set your clubs into a cart, but clean them after your round and carry them to your car. Is all this worth it? Depends what you want out of a round of golf.

CHAPTER 7

ETIQUETTE

The expression *"Golf is a gentleman's game"* may be outdated, but if you watch the sports news at night, you'll notice that you never see highlights of pro golfers engaging in fisticuffs during the heat of the battle. They don't even glare at each other. And have you noticed that there's no guy in a striped shirt controlling the action and blowing his whistle? This is because the players call penalties on themselves. It's called the *honor system*. Can you imagine? Millions of dollars at stake in each tournament and the players police themselves?

So what gives? Do all pro golfers believe in karma? Probably not. The truth is, since its birth, the sport of "playing golf" has always carried with it a set of values based on honesty, integrity, and respect for the fellow player. This set of values, also known as *golf etiquette*, is as vital to the golf experience as swinging a club. In a round of golf, you're stuck with the same three people for four hours straight, during which you must be able to focus on your game without getting in the way of theirs. When it comes right down to it, much of your performance—as well as your appreciation of the round—hinges on the behavior of the people around you. This may explain, in part, why golf is such a conservative game. With etiquette being a legacy that's centuries old and an essential part of the game, a reluctant attitude toward change is perhaps understandable.

So, there's some responsibility that comes along with picking up the game of golf. You'll be expected to carry on the tradition of good etiquette that's been handed down from generation to generation since the fifteenth century. Not moved? Think of it this way: If you don't learn proper etiquette, other golfers won't want to play with you. And that's the truth. If you don't believe it, wait until you play a round with somebody—and you will—who doesn't know how to conduct him- or herself on a golf course. You'll be distracted, annoyed, and frustrated, and you'll want to do anything to make sure none of your future playing partners ever feels the same way about you. Instead of learning from mistakes, however, brush up on your etiquette before you play. Your partners will appreciate it, and ultimately, you'll enjoy the game more yourself.

There are four ingredients to good etiquette: pace of play, taking care of your playing partners, taking care of the golf course, and knowing the rules. We'll take them one by one.

PACE OF PLAY

Without a doubt, the biggest problem on the average American golf course is slow play. Unfortunately, it's all too common to go to a golf course, public or private, during a summer weekend, and find yourself embroiled in a five-hour round. Even if the weather is perfect and the scenery breathtaking, five hours is too long to spend on the golf course. Why? Because the average golfer hits the ball about ninety times during a round, and it takes less than two seconds to swing a golf club. So most of that five hours will be spent waiting. Waiting is a problem. It throws off your rhythm. Once you hit the golf ball, you want to hit it again, and if you have to spend five minutes waiting for the group in front of you to get out of range every time, you're going to get annoyed.

What's perhaps even more annoying is that on your typical golf course, where there may be as many as forty-five groups—nearly two hundred golfers—at one time, you can usually count the ones responsible for the slow pace on two hands. To state the obvious, you don't want to be one of these people. Not only does slow play alienate you from fellow players, it also does damage to your game. Good golf is played at a brisk, upbeat pace. This is not to say you should be jogging between shots, but your energy must be up if you're going to perform consistently. Playing slow—dawdling between shots, overpreparing, wasting time—lets energy drain out of you, and makes it difficult for you to string together a series of good shots.

More than anything else, playing at a good pace means always being ready to hit when it's your turn. (It's your turn

Save time by preparing to hit your next shot while your partners play theirs.

when your ball is the farthest one from the hole; more on this later.) This sounds like a simple rule but it's the one most often violated. Here's what usually happens: Four players tee off on the first hole. Instead of each player going to his or her ball and preparing to hit it by selecting the proper club and going through whatever preshot routine he or she may have, all four players go to the first ball. They wait for the first player to pick a club, go through a preshot routine, and hit the ball. Then they move on to the second ball and repeat the process. Minutes pass between shots when the four could conceivably be hitting seconds apart.

This example points to rule #1 of fast play. *After everybody tees off, don't be a spectator. Go to your own ball.* The exception is if your ball is directly between one of your partners' balls and the hole. If you're sharing a cart with another player and he hits a longer drive than you, have him drop you off at your ball. Choose your club, then send him ahead, with the cart, to his ball. As you're hitting your shot, he prepares to hit his. As he

THE MULTIPLE CLUB/CART TRICK

Here's an interesting problem: You're in a cart. Your partner is farthest from the hole, facing a particularly difficult shot from behind a tree—one that's going to require some thought. You're twenty yards ahead, in the fairway. What do you do? Well, the quickest move is to drop off your partner and let him do his thing while you drive to your ball and prepare to do yours. But your partner isn't ready for that yet. He can't decide whether to hit a low 5-iron around the trees or an 8-iron over them. On the other hand, he could just pitch out with a wedge, so you'd better just wait there with the cart while he makes up his mind, right? Wrong. As soon as the cart reaches the ball, your partner should have an idea of what his options are. Let him take his 5-iron, 8-iron, and wedge

out of the bag and make his decisions while you drive ahead with the cart.

Be ready to do things like this often when you ride. Even though carts move faster than humans, they have a knack for actually slowing up play if not used wisely. This is especially true at resorts that feature a single paved cart path running up the side of the fairway and require carts to stay on this path at all times. In this case you must park the cart on the path, walk over to your ball, hit it, and walk back. Because your walk may be a long one—you won't know exactly how long until you get to your ball—it's smart to take two or three clubs with you so you're covered. The last thing you (or the players in the group behind you) want to see happen is you walking fifty yards to your ball, realizing you have the wrong club, and walking back to the cart for a replacement.

hits his shot, you walk forward to rejoin him at the cart when he's finished. A well paced foursome plays in a flowing, integrated fashion, which brings us to rule #2 of fast play. *Do most of your preshot preparation while other players are hitting.* This includes selecting your club, lining up your shot, taking practice swings—anything that doesn't distract the golfer playing the shot. This rule is especially important on the green. There's no reason why three golfers should wait while the fourth lines up his putt from four angles. Line it up while it isn't your turn, so that when it *is* your turn, you're playing a stroke and not preparing to do so.

A good measuring point: From the moment that it becomes your turn, it should never take you more than twenty seconds to hit the ball. If it does, either you're not making enough of the time when others are playing, or you're faced with an incredibly difficult shot that requires extra thought and preparation. In the latter case, employ rule #3 of fast play: *If you need extra time to prepare for a shot, feel free to waive the order-of-play rule.* That is, if you've got a tough shot and you're farthest from the hole, let the players who are closer hit while you prepare. That way they're not waiting on you.

If slow play is hell, then practice swings are surely the devil himself. These preparatory passes at an imaginary ball are the time—consuming crutches of the beginning golfer. Unsure of what exactly to do on an upcoming shot, the beginning golfer often falls back on a series of practice swings in the hope of finding a feeling he can repeat for the real thing. In theory this is fine, but realistically, practice swings are much different from the real thing precisely because there is no ball to be hit. The damage they do to the overall pace of play on a golf course far outweighs any help they provide to an individual golfer. Another thing: If you're searching for a swing by making practice swings before you hit a shot, your head is in the wrong place. You're thinking about swinging rather than playing.

Remember the distinction: Swinging is about swinging, playing is about moving a ball from the tee to the hole. So, rule #4 of fast play is simple: *Keep practice swings to a bare minimum.* And again, if you absolutely must practice, do it discreetly, while somebody else is hitting. When it's your turn, just get up and hit the ball. It may be scary without those practice swings to hold onto, but ultimately, it'll lead you to better play.

A few more rules:

Rule #5: *Leave your bag between the hole and the next tee.* When it's time to putt, take the time to place your bag or cart on a line between the hole and the next tee, so that when you're finished you don't have to cross down to the front of the green to grab your clubs while players in the fairway behind you wait.

Rule #6: *Mark down scores on the next tee.* If you're keeping score for your group, don't mark down the scores on the green of the hole you're finishing. Wait until you get onto the next tee, then fill out the scorecard while everybody else hits.

Rule #7: *Don't get too attached to your golf ball.* That is, be willing to part with it if your drive soars into thick woods. If you think you have a legitimate chance to find it, take a quick look and enlist one other member of your foursome to help. Let the rest get ready to hit their own shots. If you don't find your ball within a minute, give up. (What to do next is covered in the rules section later in this chapter.) The actual *Rules of*

THE SEVEN RULES OF FAST PLAY

1. After everybody tees off, don't be a spectator. Go to your own ball.
2. Do most of your preshot preparation while other play-ers are hitting.
3. If you need extra time to prepare for a shot, feel free to waive the order-of-play rule.
4. Keep practice swings to a bare minimum.
5. Leave your bag between the hole and the next tee.
6. Mark down scores on the next tee.
7. Don't get too attached to your golf ball.

Golf gives you five minutes to look for a lost ball, which is fine for tournament play, but on a crowded course during the weekend, a five-minute search conducted by an entire foursome is like an overturned tractor trailer during rush hour: gridlock material.

TAKING CARE OF YOUR PLAYING PARTNERS

When you watch golf on TV, you'll notice that the announcers are often whispering. "Johnny, he's got an unbelievably bad lie here. It'll be a miracle if he gets the ball close...." They're whispering to make sure the players don't hear them, not because they're saying bad things but because the players require silence when they make their shots.

This may sound finicky, but a golf swing is something that requires special concentration, and you don't have to be a pro to get distracted by somebody talking in the middle of your backswing. Taking care of your playing partners means making sure that you're playing up to speed, and that they can play their shots without distraction. Aside from not talking, this means no club-rattling, coin-jingling, Velcro15-ripping (on your glove), or idling of the cart. Stillness is also important. If you're within a twenty-foot radius of your partner while he's playing a shot, don't move. Even though his head is down, he'll see you out of the corner of his eye, breaking his focus. Lastly, where you stand is important. Maintain a distance of a good ten feet or so. Players are different but many get distracted if you stand directly alongside them or behind them, on their target line. The best places to stand while someone plays are 45 degrees to the back left or back right of him. This is especially true on the green: It may be tempting to stand directly behind someone's ball or the hole as he putts, but it's a no no, a major distractor.

Specialties of the Green: Everything gets a little more

Find a place to stand that is the least distracting to your partners.

delicate when you get onto the green, so you have to be more careful. The above principles—silence and stillness—hold true, but there are a few extra things you must know:

Awareness of where you step—If you wear golf shoes, remember that they have metal spikes, which make holes. Obviously these will be imperceptible in the fairway and rough, but on the short grass of the green spike marks alter the surface and can change the way a putt rolls to the hole. What's more, even if you're not wearing spikes, your footprints will leave depressions in the green that can also alter the line of a putt. There's nothing you can do about this except take care not to step in other players' lines. If you're crossing the green, take the long route around their balls or step over their lines as you go. Because all players have to walk to the hole to pick up their balls, it's a good idea to avoid doing a lot of walking in that area, which gets beat up enough as it is. Even if you're playing on bumpy, patchy greens, show your playing partners the courtesy of staying off of their lines. It may not make a real difference, but it's gracious and good practice for the times when you play on the smooth greens where it will count.

Marking your ball—You and your playing partner have both reached the green. He's twenty feet away from the hole, you're ten; but your ball is directly between his and the hole. Years ago, your partner would have had to somehow try to putt around your ball, but today the Rules of Golf allow you to place a mark on the green and pick up your ball. Here's the procedure:

You can buy specially made ball markers—little disks with spikes in them so they stick on the green—but you can mark your ball with just about anything: a coin, a tee, a marble, whatever you want. The rules provide for this but, just to make it

Proper procedure for moving a mark, as requested by your playing partner.

easy on yourself and your partner, use a coin. Standing so the ball is between yourself and the hole, place the coin on the ground just behind the ball. Now you can pick up the ball and clean it, put it in your pocket, whatever. When you're ready to hit your putt, place the ball back where it was, and pick up the coin.

Moving your mark—Occasionally your mark will lie directly on the line on which your playing partner intends to roll his putt. In this case, since he doesn't want his ball deflected by your mark (even a dime can alter the path of a rolling ball), he can ask you to move the mark while he putts. Under the rules, if he asks, you are obliged to do so, then replace your mark in its original position when he's finished. There's a standard procedure for this:

Suppose your partner asks you to move your mark to the right of his line. Pick out an object at an approximate right angle to the hole, such as a tree or sprinkler head. Place your putter on the ground so the heel is next to your mark and the toe points at the object you've chosen. Then pick up the mark and replace it next to the toe of your putter. You've just moved it one putterhead length. Remove your club while your partner putts. When he's finished, place the putter back on the ground with the toe next to your mark and pointing at your chosen object. Pick up the mark and replace it next to the heel. This should be the mark's original position. Don't forget to move the mark back or it will cost you an extra stroke. Usually moving the mark one putterhead length is enough, but occasionally your partner may ask you to move it two. In this case, follow the same procedure—just repeat it.

One warning: You must mark your ball before moving it. Otherwise, if you move your ball, you'll receive a penalty. Be sure to mark it first.

a: replacing a divot   b: raking a bunker   c: repairing a ball mark

TAKING CARE OF THE GOLF COURSE

There's a reason why some golf courses are lush and green and others are brown and patchy: Some are well taken care of, others aren't. It's not just the maintenance staffs that are responsible. The golfers who play these courses deserve equal credit or blame. The fact is, weather isn't all that dishes out wear and tear on a golf course. Golfers do, too. While there's little you can do to prevent this, there are measures you can take to reduce the damage. They're simple tasks that should become part of your playing routine. They'll be expected of you if you play at a friend's club, and if you have a course you play regularly yourself, you'll want to keep it in the best condition possible.

Replacing divots—When a clubhead hits the grass at the bottom of the swing, it doesn't bounce. It cuts out a sliver of grass and dirt, leaving what's called a *divot*. Fairways are green; they're pretty. Divots are brown with sediments and sometimes worms in them; they're not pretty. For the sake of aesthetics—as well as the fact that hitting out of divots is a pain in the neck for the players behind you—replace all your divots. Just go get that little carpet of fairway and put it back where it came from. This is not just a symbolic gesture, either. Replacing the divot gives the grass a chance to fuse with its original roots, so it grows back healthier and faster. A replaced divot will be untraceable in a matter of a couple weeks; an unreplaced divot takes months to grow back. The exception to this is those courses, found mostly in the South, that have fairways made of a special grass called *bermuda*. Ordinarily you don't replace bermuda grass divots, because the grass doesn't re-fuse with its roots. However, the courses—usually resorts that require carts—provide little buckets of sandy fertilizer with which you can fill the divots. Bermuda grass takes root quickly in this mixture. Either way, though, the concept is the same: Don't take a divot without repairing it.

Raking sand bunkers—Hitting out of the sand is difficult enough; you'll find it nearly impossible if your ball is lying in somebody's footprint. Because sand is generally soft, the process of taking your stance and hitting your shot leaves a bit of a mess. If by the end of the day all the players who hit the ball out of the sand did nothing about the condition of the bunker, the place would look like a war zone. That's why you'll usually find one or more rakes lying around the edges of a bunker. They're used to smooth out the sand after you've played your shot.

In the interest of time, take the rake with you when you enter the bunker to approach your ball. Always enter and leave the bunker from the back—that is, the side farthest from the green. Most bunkers slope upward toward the green, and walking up or down this slope causes mini-sand avalanches that leave the bunker face raw and hard. When you reach your ball, put down the rake so it's out of the way, and hit your shot. Then rake the spot from which you hit the ball, as well as your footprints leading into the bunker. If you exit the way you came in, you can wipe out both sets of footprints at once.

Fixing ball marks—Depending on how hard the green's surface is and how long the shot was, a ball hitting the green from approximately sixty or more yards away will leave a dimple, or *ball mark*. Like divots, these marks, if unattended to, damage the green and become obstacles for other players' putts. If you consider that a dime can alter the path of a rolling ball, imagine what a $\frac{3}{4}$ inch-deep pit can do. You'll find that the greens you really enjoy playing on have few or no ball marks—because they've all been repaired—and roll relatively true, like a pool table. The greens that frustrate you, on the other hand, will have plenty of unrepaired ball marks, and getting your ball to the hole can be like playing pinball. Every golfer has to contribute in order to keep the greens in good shape. The traditional rallying cry is "fix your ball mark plus one other," and it's not a bad practice. A repaired ball mark will look like new after a couple days; leaving a ball mark unrepaired kills the grass within, and it may take weeks to grow back. The trick is knowing how. Many well-intentioned golfers do even further damage to the green by repairing ball marks improperly. For the sake of the course, your playing partners, and yourself, learn the right way.

Like ball-markers, you can buy specially made ball-mark-repair tools, but a tee is just as effective. If you are out of tees, you can use a key or similar object.

Fixing a ball mark is a process of closing a hole, not smoothing out a dent. That's the usual mistake. Often golfers will stick the tee into the ground and try to lift the hole back to the surface, using the tee as a lever. This lifting action breaks the roots of the grass, so that although the hole may be gone, the grass within it dies, leaving a brown patch. Rather than trying to lift the center of the hole upward, though, fixing a ball mark should be more like pinching the edges of the hole together until they touch. To do this, stick the tee in the ground just outside the edge of the ball mark, then press the tee toward the center of the hole. You'll see the edge move inward. Make your way around the hole with the tee, pushing the edges in closer until they touch and the hole is covered up. This way the hole is closed and no roots are broken, giving the grass a chance to fuse and grow.

Other greenside manners—To preserve the surface of the green, be careful with everything you do upon it. Never leave your bag or pull cart on the green; always leave it at least a few feet outside the fringe. Be careful with the flagstick, as well. When you take it out of the hole, either lay it gently on the green so it's out of everybody's way, or lay it on the fringe. Never drop it on the green; it will leave marks. For the same reason, running or jumping on the green—for whatever purpose —is a bad idea. Any intense foot action will result in extra-deep footprints and severe spike marks. Do your acrobatics in the fairway or rough.

KNOWING THE RULES

If it isn't immediately clear how large a part knowing the rules is of good etiquette, imagine playing baseball with someone who doesn't understand that once you're out, you stop running. What a drag: He grounds out to the shortstop, the throw beats him by a mile, but he tries to stretch it into a double anyway. He slides into second, nobody is there to tag him, so he gets up and starts running for third. He makes a wide turn at the corner and hightails it for home plate, where he makes a headfirst dive. . . .

You get the idea. In any sport, the rules dictate the play. What's more, in golf you are your own referee, so it's even more important that you have a solid grasp of the rules. The game's rule maker, the United States Golf Association (USGA), publishes a booklet containing the complete Rules of Golf each year. It's recommended reading for all golfers, from novice to expert. The only trouble is, it's a good 140 pages long, which is a pretty big homework assignment, especially if you haven't even been to class yet.

So, although you should make plans to start working your way through an official rulebook sometime soon, (available at your local pro shop, or write to the USGA at Golf House, Far Hills, NJ 07931), it's perhaps unfair to expect you to devour all that information before stepping onto a golf course. Still, you must have a basic set of rules to go by. Here, then, is a condensed version:

TEN BASIC RULES OF PLAY

1. A stroke is a stroke is a stroke. Every time you swing at the ball with the intention of hitting it, it counts as a stroke. There are no do-overs or don't-counts. If somebody yelled during your backswing or your ball was in an "unfair" lie, count the stroke anyway. No matter how many bad breaks you experience during a round, you'll get your fair share of good breaks, too, so it will all balance out.

2. Play the ball as it lies. This one's basically self explanatory: Wherever your ball is in play (not out of bounds or in a water hazard; in these cases, see rules 6 and 7 below), that's where you must hit it from. No rolling it over into a better lie. The exceptions: areas marked as ground under repair, and free-drop areas, such as cart paths or sprinkler heads. In these cases, move the ball to the nearest point of relief that's no closer to the hole, and play from there.

3. Tee the ball between the markers. Tee-markers are there for a reason; pay attention to their location. Your ball must be teed anywhere from the line between the two markers to two club lengths in back of it. Your feet don't have to be between the markers as you play your shot, but if your ball is at all ahead of the markers, it's a one stroke penalty.

4. Whoever is farthest from the hole plays first. As stated earlier, however, the player who's up can waive this rule and allow other players to hit before him in the interest of time. Be ready to waive this rule to keep the pace moving.

5. Whoever had the lowest score on the previous hole hits first on the next tee. This is called *having the honor*. The order of play on each tee is determined by the scores on the previous hole, low to high. If there are ties, go back to the scores of the hole before that, and so on.

6. If your shot goes anywhere near out of bounds or risks being lost, hit a provisional shot. This is not a do-over. Suppose your tee shot is veering toward the out-of-bounds stakes on the right side of the hole. You're not sure whether it's in or out. The rules state that if you hit a ball out of bounds, you must take a penalty stroke, then retee from the original spot. This is called a *stroke and distance penalty*. Rather than checking on the status of your drive, then having to walk all the way back to the tee to hit again, play a second drive right away, just in case. The same goes for a shot that flies into heavily wooded areas that might make finding the ball difficult.

WHAT IS A DROP?

In any situation where you must put the ball into play without either placing it on a tee or hitting it with a golf club—such as removing it from a cart path or a water hazard—the rules dictate that you must drop it, rather than placing it. That's to ensure that you don't have a choice of what your lie will be. To drop, stand facing the hole, extend your arm to the side, and let the ball fall from your hand. Wherever it comes to rest is where you play your next stroke from (assuming the ball finishes in play; if not, you must drop again).

By hitting a provisional ball, you're covering your tracks. Understand that if your first ball *is* lost or out of bounds, your provisional ball counts as your third stroke of the hole, because of the one stroke penalty.

If you're playing in formal competition and your provisional ball also flies out of bounds, you just repeat the process until you get a shot in play. However, if you're just playing a casual round, don't hit more than one provisional. In the interest of speedy play, drop a ball near the spot where your ball went out of bounds and play from there. Penalize yourself another stroke and continue.

Taking a drop

7. Water hazards are not stroke-and-distance penalties. You've hit your tee shot into the lake by the right side of the fairway. You have the option of taking a penalty stroke and hitting another shot from the tee—but this would be a waste of time and, in all but the most unusual cases, a more difficult shot. Instead, take a penalty stroke and drop the ball at the approximate point at which it entered the water hazard. This means you'll be hitting your third shot from next to the lake, rather than from the tee.

> **Speedy play tip:** The Rules of Golf mandate that stroke-and-distance penalties must be taken for lost balls or balls hit out of bounds. In formal competition, yes. In your casual rounds, though, you'll find it easier and faster to play lost and out of bounds balls as hazards: Take a penalty stroke and drop the ball where it entered the wooded or out-of-bounds area. Be sure to come to an agreement with your playing partners on this policy before your round.

8. Don't ground the club in a sand trap. Grounding the club means letting it touch the ground at any time other than ball impact. Why can't you touch the club to the ground in a sand trap? Because this would give you the opportunity to draw all kinds of helpful alignment lines in the sand; in addition, a bunker is a hazard, and the rules stipulate that you may not ground your club in a hazard. This includes water hazards, so on the odd occasion when you find your ball partially submerged in the edge of a lake or pond, yet still hittable, don't touch the water with your club until impact.

9. Don't putt with the flagstick in. The flagstick is a double edged sword; it can prevent some putts that would ordinarily go in from doing so, and allow some that wouldn't to drop. Regardless, if you hit the flagstick

Hold flag
against flagstick

Pull stick out
of hole as ball
approaches

Shadow
away from
hole

Tending a flagstick

with a putted ball it's a one-stroke penalty. The exception comes if you're putting onto the green from off its surface—say, from the fringe. In this case, you may leave the flagstick in. Now, suppose you are on the green, but seventy feet from the hole, and you can't really see it without the flagstick? Ask one of your playing partners to tend the flagstick. He will stand beside it while you line up and make your stroke; while your ball is rolling to the hole he'll take the flagstick out. If, however, your ball is off the green, you may not have the flagstick tended for you. Either leave it in, or take it out.

Additionally, you should know that it's a penalty if your putt hits the flagstick at any time—even when it's not in the hole. So, when you take out the flagstick, be sure to lay it down in some out-of-the-way place, like the fringe.

10. Don't let your ball hit another player's ball on the green. One of the main reasons to mark a ball is that if you putt your ball on the green and it hits another player's, you'll receive a one stroke penalty. In this case, the other player replaces his ball at its original spot; you must play yours from wherever it lies, and add the one stroke. Be sure to also ask your playing partners to mark their balls if they lie anywhere close to yours, or to where yours might roll.

Remember, these ten rules are the least you should know; they're designed to let you get around the course without making any major mistakes. Do take the time to read the USGA's rulebook. It will give you a better understanding of why the rules exist as they do, and how the entire game is played.

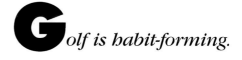

CHAPTER 8

Golf is habit-forming.

It takes just a few rounds for the addiction to

set in, in the form of an insatiable desire to

improve. Golfers who shoot 100 would give

anything to break 90. When they finally do,

they set their sights on 80. This desire is a major part of being a golfer, and of why the game has exploded in popularity over the last ten years. As soon as you try it, you not only want more, you want to master it. The reason? Aside from its obvious benefits— exercise, relaxation, time in the outdoors—golf teases you with glimpses of your own potential brilliance. In every round you'll hit some bad shots, you'll hit some fair shots, and then you'll hit a couple shots that are so good they'll surprise you. They'll give you an idea of what your game could be like if you really worked at it—if you got rid of that slice, or that three-putting problem, or whatever it is that ails you. So you'll resolve to keep playing and try to get better, to take your game to the next level.

But how do you go about this? Frankly, most golfers get suckered. Instead of getting good instruction from qualified people and putting in significant practice time, the majority of the golfing public invests its money and hopes into books, magazine articles, equipment, videos, and instructional gadgets that promise improvement. No sport has a larger market for instruction than golf. None comes close. This is not to say the aforementioned items are worthless, but nothing replaces the real McCoy: one on one instruction from a Professional Golfer's Association (PGA) professional, and solid practice time on your own. Obviously, it takes less time and money to pick up a golf magazine each month than it does to take a lesson, but this may do more damage to your game than good. Remember: Getting worse is easier in golf than any other sport. If you really want to improve—and feed your addiction—you need a game plan that keeps you on the proper path and doesn't let you stray into the land of bad habits. We all know what happened to Dorothy when she left the Yellow Brick Road. Flying monkeys. They're everywhere.

So, rule #1 of how to get better at golf is, Don't look for the quick fix. Books, videos, and magazines are fine; just make sure they supplement your learning curriculum and don't become the curriculum itself. As a beginning golfer, getting a good grasp of the fundamentals is priority one. For this you need hands on instruction, from someone who can physically put you into the proper positions so you know exactly what they feel like. You need a teacher with a trained eye, one who can spot the flaws in your swing and who knows how to get rid of them. That means you must see a PGA Teaching Professional. A PGA pro is trained and certified to teach golf, and—as complicated as the swing can be—you want yourself in an expert's hands. Don't settle for less.

LEARNING

You have a number of options when it comes to how you'll learn the game. You can either take one-on-one lessons with a PGA teaching pro (there's one at just about every course), or take group lessons with a pro, or go to a golf school for a few days. Each method has its pros and cons; a close look at your expectations will reveal the best choice for you.

PGA OF AMERICA VS. PGA TOUR

Tell a person not completely familiar with the game that he or she should see a PGA pro and he might ask, "You mean like Jack Nicklaus?" Not quite. Officially, yes, Jack Nicklaus and all those pros you see on TV are members of the Professional Golfers' Association, but they're members of a part of the PGA called the PGA Tour, which is a league of golfers who make their living at the game. The PGA of America is much larger than the PGA Tour, and is made up of professionals who make their living teaching golf, rather than playing it. They are also PGA pros—and pretty good players, too—but they're not members of the PGA Tour.

One-on-one lessons—This is the most intensive type of instructional session. It's just you and a pro for up to an hour, with complete focus on how to improve your game. It's the fastest road to improvement, and has only one drawback: It's not for the meek. Probably the first thing the pro will say to you is, "Okay, let's see you hit a few balls." If situations like this put pressure on you and make you uncomfortable, one-on-one lessons may not be your best choice—at least not initially. You should expect that during the course of your first few lessons—and probably more than a few after that—there will be periods of time when you will be completely inept. This is par for the course (if you will). You must be willing to fail in order to get better. If you don't like the idea of doing this in a one-on-one situation, that's okay. Group lessons will probably be more your speed.

If, however, the intimacy of a one-on-one lesson doesn't bother you, jump right in and take a few. One lesson is fine, but when you're starting the game, it's good to monitor your progress closely. This way the pro can make sure that his or her instruction truly "takes" with you and that you don't develop any bad habits early on. Many teaching professionals offer a package of three lessons; this is a good place to start.

Before you actually put down your money, however, be sure you and the pro have taken the time to familiarize yourselves with each other. He should know your level of play and what you're looking to get out of the lessons (here's a hint: a solid grasp of the fundamentals!). He should also tell you a little about himself: what kind of player he prefers working with, his teaching methods and philosophies, and so on. A good teacher/student relationship can have an enormously positive effect on your learning process.

Group lessons—The con here is that, with more people for the pro to watch, you'll get less individualized attention. The pro: When you're going through a particularly painful period of ineptitude, you can just glance over at your fellow students and take comfort in the fact that they're going through the exact same thing.

The ideal way to set up a group lesson or a series of group

lessons is to organize a few friends of ability similar to your own, and approach the pro as a group. If none of your friends plays golf, tell the pro you're interested in a group lesson; he'll pair you up with a group of golfers at your skill level, if one exists. If the pro doesn't teach any groups and you don't have a group of your own, you may have to just suck it up and go for the one-on-one experience.

Again, I recommend that you take a series of lessons at the outset, especially because you'll be getting less attention in a group setting, and improvement may take more time to accomplish.

Golf schools —This is a different kind of experience altogether. At a golf school, you set aside two to seven days and devote them almost completely to golf. It's a crash course no matter what level of player you are. This is not to say a school isn't appropriate for the beginning player; in fact, it's a great way to introduce yourself to the game. How better to learn whether you like a game than to live and breathe it from dawn to dusk every day? Not only that, you get to live and breathe it at a nice

The golf school practice tee.

resort in a warm, pretty setting. The instruction is usually top notch as well. Golf schools get most of their business from word of mouth testimonials, so you can count on the pros being first rate.

A typical day at a golf school starts early. Breakfast is served between 7:30 and 9 A.M. (Some schools include some or all meals in the package, others don't; do your research.) You're on the lesson tee by 10, get instruction from 10 to 12, break for lunch, then head back to the lesson tee from 1 to 3. The focus is usually on the full swing, but expect the short game and putting to be covered as well. Usually you have the option to go play the course in the late afternoon, after the formal instruction is over.

The biggest drawback to the golf-school experience is the student: teacher ratio: It's almost never better than 4:1, and usually more like 6:1. This means that, although you'll spend more time working on your game, you'll get less individualized instruction. In each day that you spend at a golf school, you may get forty-five minutes to an hour of one-on-one attention from a golf professional. The rest of the time you'll either be on your own or receiving instruction as part of a group. Don't expect to digest a lifetime's worth of fundamental golf instruction during one course, even if it's a week long. Too many things will be going on at once for you to leave with all of them imprinted on your subconscious. Golf school is, however, a complete and fun way to introduce yourself to the game—and some other players as well.

SEVEN OF THE BEST GOLF SCHOOLS AND WHY THEY'RE GREAT

No matter which school you attend, chances are pretty good that you'll stay at a nice resort with a good golf course and receive excellent instruction. There are a few schools, however, that distinguish themselves:

1. Nicklaus/Flick Golf Schools (11780 U.S. Highway One, North Palm Beach, FL 33408-9809; (800) 642-5528)— Jack Nicklaus himself doesn't teach here, but one of his mentors, the indefatigable Jim Flick, does, and he's one of the best alive. Flick believes that special care must be taken with the beginning golfer to make sure he or she gets off on the right foot. He and his staff of teaching pros will do everything they can to give you a good feel for the game. You'll live well, too. Nicklaus/Flick holds schools at various locations around the country, all of them beautiful, high-end destinations: Palm Beach, Florida; Pebble Beach, California; Scottsdale, Arizona; and Boyne Highlands, Michigan, among others.

2. _Golf Digest_ Instruction Schools (5520 Park Avenue, Box 395, Trumbull, CT 06611-0395; (800) 243-6121)— The great thing about the schools created by the popular magazine is that they really take care of you. Included in the tuition are transportation to and from the airport, all meals, and all rounds of golf, so once you get off the plane you have nothing to worry about (except gripping the club properly and everything that goes along with it).

3. The Dave Pelz Short Game School (The Boca Raton Resort & Club, Box 5025, Boca Raton, FL 33431 0825; (800) 833 7370)—As the name implies, the Pelz school devotes itself entirely to the short game: pitching, chipping, sand play, and putting. If you think leaving the full swing out of the curriculum is skimping, don't. Ask any pro what the fastest way to improve your scores is and he'll tell you, working on your short game. More than half the strokes you take during any given round are on or around the green. Although the short game is usually the last thing the new golfer develops, it's also the least challenging physically, in terms of strength and flexibility. A solid grounding in its fundamentals will supercharge your improvement process.

There's an added bonus to learning the short game early. Pitching, chipping, putting—these are all shots that require *touch,* the ability to sense how hard you must swing a club to hit the ball a given distance or trajectory. Immersing yourself in the short game will teach you touch, which in turn will help your full swing immensely. Touch is the missing element in most amateurs' golf swings.

4. John Jacobs Golf Schools (7825 East Redfield Road, Scottsdale, AZ 85260-6977; (800) 472-5007)—It's common to run across teachers who preach certain methods of teaching, as in "Joe Golfpro's Patented Momentum Method, the easiest and most natural way to swing a golf club." At John Jacobs, however, students undergo no such jumping through hoops, and that's what makes the schools great. Jacobs doesn't espouse any particular method; he takes whatever you have and helps you make it work.

It's a philosophy that seems to be effective; Jacobs's schools receive consistent raves from the students, especially beginners. Although based in Arizona, John Jacobs holds more than eight hundred schools at thirty different locations worldwide.

5. The Ben Sutton Golf Academy (Box 9199, Canton, OH 44711; (800) 225-6923)—There's a big difference between hitting balls on a practice range and playing an actual round. On the range, your focus is usually on the swing and what it looks or feels like; on the course, your focus is on getting the ball into the hole, which, after all, is the object of the game. You can have a beautiful swing and still be a mediocre golfer if you don't know how to score (a separate, developable skill). The Ben Sutton Golf Academy is one of the few schools that asks students, regardless of ability, to focus on scoring first and swing mechanics second. In addition to a 27-hole resort layout at Sun City, Florida, the Sutton School has its own 9-hole practice course on site. The majority of instruction time is spent on the practice course, working on the actual playing situations you'll encounter during a typical round.

6. Doral Golf Learning Center with Jim McLean (4400 Northwest 87th Avenue, Miami, FL 33178; (800) 72-DORAL)—It's only appropriate that just a few minutes' drive from high-profile South Beach is the home of Jim McLean, teacher to the stars. In addition to working with Tour pros Tom Kite, Brad Faxon, and Peter Jacobsen, McLean has been guru to names like Stallone and Dr. J, among many others. He's a big shot, but he deserves the recognition; few teachers have spent more time studying the golf swing and the art of teaching it. With a solid supporting cast of teaching professionals, McLean's Learning Center is on the cutting edge of golf instruction.

Doral is also pretty plush. In addition to an award-winning hotel and spa, there are 99 holes of golf, including the famed Blue Monster, which plays host to the PGA Tour's Doral-Ryder Open every year.

7. Pinehurst Golf Advantage Schools (Box 4000, Pinehurst, NC 28374; (919) 295-8128)—Three words: Location, location, and location. It's no wonder Pinehurst is the self-proclaimed golf capital of the world: Golf courses clearly belong here. They wander under towering pines and around sleepy lakes and ponds as if these weren't human-made. It's so charming that attending the Advantage Schools may feel more like returning to summer camp than visiting a highbrow resort. Nongolfing family members will enjoy coming here: In addition to a great school with some of the best courses in the world, there are also on-site tennis, horseback riding, and water sports.

The gem of the entire complex is Pinehurst #2, the legendary golf course designed by Donald Ross. *Golf Magazine* routinely ranks it among the top ten golf courses in the world, and, for an extra fee, students of the Advantage Schools can play the elegant layout. Be sure to bring your "A" game, though: #2 is just as hard as it is beautiful.

Regardless of which school you choose, be prepared to spend money. Golf schools are, as a rule, pricey compared to private lessons. At Doral, for example, five days with Jim McLean will cost you close to $3000. Many schools are less expensive, a few cost more. For a more complete listing of golf schools around the country, try Shaw's *Guide to Golf Schools and Camps,* which is very comprehensive.

In addition to price, there are a few other questions you should ask before making your decision:

What's the maximum class size? This is important; at some schools—John Jacobs, for one—classes can balloon to more than thirty people. Even if there are a lot of instructors, a huge class size can leave you lost in the shuffle.

What's the student:teacher ratio? The smaller the ratio, the more personalized attention you get. If the ratio is greater than 6:1, things could get out of hand.

What's included? Meals, transportation to and from the airport, greens fees, cart fees—all must be accounted for. Be sure you know whether they're your responsibility or the school's before you compare prices.

How far in advance do I need to book?

What are the policies and facilities available for non-golfers? Your spouse and/or family will appreciate knowing this. Some schools offer a vacation for the entire family; others are just golf, more golf, and only golf.

PRACTICING

Taking a few lessons or going to a golf school is a big step toward improving your game, but it's only a beginning. The real work will come afterward, when you apply what you've learned from the PGA pro on your own. This means plenty of on-course play, and, just as importantly, of practice. If you groaned reading that last sentence, you're not alone. Few amateurs take lessons on a consistent basis; if they do, fewer regularly practice what they've learned. Unfortunately, though, there's just no substitute for practice. It takes time out of your schedule but, without it, you simply won't get better. If that's fine with you, then you can skip practice with a clear conscience; golf, however, has a way of driving you crazy if you don't see improvement. Chances are you'll be unhappy with your game if you don't work on it.

But be of good cheer. Practicing golf isn't as tedious as playing scales on the piano; in fact, it can be fun, if done correctly. But where to go? Ideally, you'd go to your local course, and there'd be a driving range with grass tees, a practice putting green, and a practice green devoted to pitching, chipping, and sand play. If this is available to you, consider yourself blessed. More likely you'll find that—if your course has a driving range at all—the tees are Astroturf mats; although it may have a practice putting green, short game practice areas are rare. If your course doesn't have a driving range, you'll have to go to your local driving range—a facility for practice only, without a golf course—to practice your swing. Putting greens and short-game

Practicing the short game is the quickest way to lower your scores.

areas are even rarer here. This is not meant to discourage you. Although Astroturf isn't the real thing, you can get in plenty of good work hitting off it, and you don't need a dedicated short-game area to practice your chipping and pitching. With a little imagination, you can practice your short game anywhere you find grass and a little space. Just pick a target and go to town. Here are a few guidelines to help you get the most out of your practice sessions:

Come prepared—Don't just go the practice range and whack away at a bucket of balls. You won't get a lot out of that, and the hour that you somehow set aside for yourself during the week will be wasted. Instead, have a game plan for each practice session, a mental list of a couple things to work on and accomplish in the time you've allotted for yourself. Look at your last lesson: What were some of the things your pro worked on with you? Grip, stance, alignment, turn? Whatever they were, choose a couple and devote a chunk of your time on the practice tee to working on them. Here's a good way to break down your session: Get yourself loose and warmed up for fifteen minutes; spend half an hour working on two fundamentals from your last lesson; then spend fifteen more minutes whacking away, because you can't deny yourself completely. That's an hour's worth of work. If you stick to the schedule, it'll be over before you know it, and you might want to stretch it to two.

Don't just swing, hit shots—Avoid getting so locked in on your swing mechanics that you stop paying attention to where the ball is going. Even the best players in the world sometimes lose track of the fact that the object of the game is not to have a perfect swing, but to get the ball into the hole. During the time when you're whacking away, give yourself a target to hit to. Most ranges place flags at strategic locations for this purpose. Do you want the ball to go low or high? Short or long? Focusing on where the ball is going will prevent your head from whirring with numerous swing thoughts, and help you progress faster.

Give your short game equal time—It's easy to hit ball after ball on the practice range and never practice pitching, chipping, or putting. But since these make up 50 percent of the game, they need equal attention. In fact, considering how vital it is to the scoring process, your short game probably deserves *more* practice time than your full swing. If you don't have access to a practice putting green (most golf courses have one), work on your strokes at home. Your short haired carpet or rug is a very viable substitute.

Make practice a game, too—Many people don't like to practice because the challenge that playing offers isn't there. It doesn't have to be that way. You can make practice challenging, and the effect will be twofold: Not only will your sessions be more fun, but by practicing under pressure you'll train yourself to play under pressure.

Seven Games to Play When You Practice

1. Range Scorecard   Have a scorecard from a course you're familiar with handy while you hit balls. Start with the first hole;

define a fairway for yourself on the driving range, then try to hit the ball within it. Determine how far the ball went, then how many yards you still have to the green. Pick a target at the appropriate distance on the range, and try to hit the ball to it with whatever club is called for. If you hit the green, give yourself two putts and add up your score for the hole. If you miss the green, pick an appropriate target for the shot you're left with, and continue the process. Once you've finished a hole, move on to the next, until you've played all 18. "Playing a round" is a good way to focus on hitting shots rather than making a particular move with your swing.

2. All Clubs, One Target   As you continue to play golf, one of the first things you'll discover is which club it takes for you to hit the ball 150 yards. Say it's a 5-iron. On the range, then, hit your 5-iron until a shot reaches the 150-yard flag. Next pull out your 4-iron and try to hit it to the 150-yard flag. You're capable of hitting it farther, but the object is to hit it exactly 150 yards. Once you've accomplished this with your 4-iron, do the same thing with your 3-iron, then go through your fairway woods and driver, too. The game will get more difficult as it progresses. Set limits for yourself: If you fail in four shots, you have to go back to the 5-iron and start over. The purpose of this game is to teach you feel. If you can learn to control the speed of your clubhead, you're on your way to gaining control of your entire swing.

3. Closest to the Pin   This is a simple game to play with a partner. Pick one target, and each of you hit a ball to it. Whoever's closest, wins. Play for points, if you want: each win gets a point, 15 points wins the game. Change the target regularly.

4. H-O-R-S-E   Like the old basketball game, you play this one with a partner, and it's especially enjoyable when you're practicing your short game, because of the larger variety of shots to hit. For those of you who have never played, here's how it works. Player A starts by calling out a particular shot—say, a twenty-yard pitch within ten feet of the flag. If he doesn't succeed at it, it's Player B's turn to call a shot and try to hit it. If Player A hits the intended shot, though, Player B must try to do the same: a twenty-yard pitch within ten feet of the flag. If Player B misses, he gets an H. Player A then calls out a different shot and tries it, and the process repeats itself, until one player misses enough shots to spell out H-O-R-S-E.

5. Drawback   This game was developed by Dave Pelz of the aforementioned Dave Pelz Short Game School. In his research, Pelz discovered that a putted ball has the best chance of going in if it is hit hard enough to roll seventeen inches past the hole. (Seventeen inches, by the way, is half the length of the average putter. Very convenient; you'll see why.) In Drawback, you hit a ten-foot putt toward the hole. If you make it, great; move back to fifteen feet. If you miss, look closely at where the ball ended up. Is it past the hole, within a seventeen-inch radius? If so, knock it in and go back to your ten-foot putt. If not, move the ball one putter length away from the hole and try to make it. If you miss, the ball must end up within that seventeen-inch radius or you'll have to move it back another putter length. This game forces you to focus less on the line of your putt and more on its required speed. Here's a hint: When it comes to putting, speed is always more important than line. Get the speed right, and chances are you'll make the putt.

6. Eleven   A putting game for two or more, to be played on a practice green that has numerous holes. Each player starts by hitting the same twenty-foot putt; whoever finishes closest to the hole gets a point. Then each player hits a second putt. If anybody misses, the other player or players get a point. Once everybody has reached the hole, the person who won the point for closest chooses the next hole, and the process repeats itself, until one player has 11 points. If anybody sinks the first putt on any hole (it should be twenty feet or more), he or she gets 3 points. This is a complete putting game: It forces you to concentrate on hitting good lag putts, and puts pressure on your short putting stroke as well.

7. Ram, Drop, and Die   This is another solo game that works on your feel for speed. Start with a two-foot putt. Make it three times: once so it hits the back of the hole with authority; a second so it falls in the middle of the cup; and a third so it falls into the hole on its last rotation. Once you can make all three in this manner, pull the ball back to three feet and try to repeat the three different putts. Keep moving the ball back until you miss; when you do, start over at two feet. By learning to vary the speed of your putts, you'll sharpen your feel for speed, ultimately leading to more made putts on the course.

How much practice do you need? Well, there are a lot of golfers out there who will tell you that you can never get enough practice. That's debatable. There's a long-standing myth in the golf world that in order to improve, you must make all kinds of personal sacrifices and hit hundreds of balls a day. And there's an entire population of golfers who follow this advice and, unfortunately, don't get any better. Don't think you need to be obsessive about practice to improve. You just need to be consistent and smart. A couple sessions a week at the range, practicing whatever points you've worked on with your pro, will make a huge difference in your full swing. You don't need to hit hundreds of balls in these sessions. Just stay focused on what you've set out to do.

As far as your short game goes, I cannot emphasize enough: It's the key to good scoring. Practice whenever you can. Try to get to a putting green; even if you can't, you can chip and pitch in your backyard or work on your stroke in your office. Avoid the impulse to spend all your practice time whacking balls at the range. You'll get blisters and little else as far as your scorecard goes.

WARMING UP

Many golfers, regardless of ability, blur the line between practicing and warming up. Make no mistake: They're two completely different things. Practice is practice. It's a time to work on whatever your game seems to need at the moment, to be analytical, to break down your swing if you wish, to make mistakes and learn more about them. Warming up has nothing to do with this. Warming up is preparation for your upcoming round. You'll do yourself and your game a great disservice if you spend the forty five minutes or hour before you play trying to work on your swing. Practice another day, even if you're hitting the ball lousy during your warm-up. Use the time instead to make sure that your muscles are loose and that you have a feel for whatever swing you're bringing to the course that day. This way, you can step onto the first tee thinking about how you want to play the hole instead of wondering whether your swing will hold up. Having a clear, focused mind-set will make an enormous difference in your level of play.

As a rule, you should arrive at the course at least forty-five minutes before your tee time to warm up. Schedules being schedules, however, that's unfortunately not always possible. Here, then, are two warm up routines, based on available time:

The Forty-five-minute Warm-up: Start without a club. Extending your arms sideways, rotate them in small circles, gradually widening until both arms are making a windmill motion. Repeat in the reverse direction. Once your shoulders are warmed up, extend your arms straight out in front of you and turn your palms upward. From this position, try to rotate your palms outward even farther, as far as they will go. Then reverse direction and rotate your palms the other way as far as they'll go. You should feel a stretch in your forearms and wrists. Lastly, stretch your lower back by bending your knees slightly

Swinging two clubs at once to loosen up.

and letting your hands fall to your toes. Let gravity gently pull your upper body toward the ground; no bouncing.

Next take your wedge and 9-iron (the heaviest clubs in the bag) and hold them together by the grips, as if they were one club. Make slow, easy swings, letting the weight of the clubs lengthen your swing and stretch your muscles each time. Don't force it; the heavy clubs will do all the work for you.

Now you're ready to hit some balls. Start with your wedge or sand wedge. Hit three balls using half a swing, just to reorient yourself to making contact; then hit five balls using a full swing. Take your time with each one. Now drop down to your 8-iron and hit five balls. Continue moving down the set, hitting five balls with every other club until you get to your driver. Taking your time, hit five balls with serious intent, then put the club back in the bag. Finish your range session by hitting some short, easy wedges to bring a sense of touch back into your hands.

Next stop is the putting green. Drop a few balls and start by hitting long putts of twenty-five feet or more, to get a feel for distance and speed. Every five or six putts, move a bit closer to the hole, until you've gradually worked your way up to short three- or four-foot putts. Don't worry about whether you're making anything; the purpose of the putting warm-up is to get a feel for your stroke and the speed of the green. Confidence is the objective here; don't put undue pressure on yourself to perform as you warm up. For a little extra boost, end your putting session by sinking twenty one- to two-foot putts in a row. Just the sight and sound of knocking the ball into the hole repeatedly will leave an imprint of success on your mind as you begin your round.

End your warm-up by hitting a variety of chips and pitches —at the practice green (if there is one), at the putting green (if it's allowed), or at the range. Pick out targets and try to land the ball on them. The purpose of this final stage is to massage your feel one last time so it's at its highest level when you begin play.

The Ten-minute Warm-up: When time is really tight, try this routine. It can also serve as your warm-up for any practice session.

Start by making ten easy swings with your wedge and 9-iron together, to loosen up your muscles. Then hit five regular shots with your wedge, five with your 7-iron, and five with a long iron or fairway wood. End your full swings by hitting five easy drives. Twenty balls. Should take you about six minutes. Spend your last four minutes hitting putts. Start with three long ones, of over twenty-five feet, then hit three in the ten- to fifteen-foot range, and finish by hitting ten or so of under six feet. This is a bare-minimum warm-up: it won't exercise all your golfing muscles completely, but it will prepare you enough so that your clubs and swing will seem familiar to you when you start play.

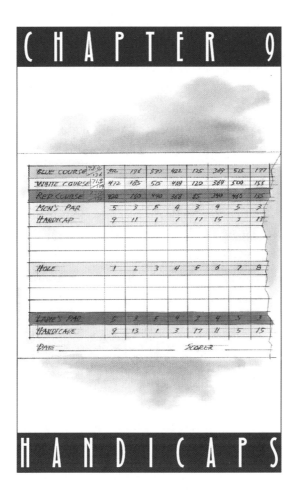

BLUE COURSE	73.0 136	512	196	530	422	125	368	515	177
WHITE COURSE	71.8 129	472	185	515	418	120	364	500	155
RED COURSE		820	160	490	368	85	340	460	135
MEN'S PAR		5	3	5	4	3	4	5	3
HANDICAP		9	11	1	7	17	15	3	13
HOLE		1	2	3	4	5	6	7	8
LADIES' PAR		5	3	5	4	3	4	5	3
HANDICAP		9	13	1	3	17	11	5	15
DATE						SCORER			

"**W**hat's your handicap?"

It's one of the most confusing questions the beginning golfer can field, yet one of the most often asked. "Take your pick," the old, joking response goes. "Driving, iron play, short game, or putting." But handicaps are serious things, and—although a mystery to many—one of golf's greatest inventions.

Your *handicap* doesn't refer to any disability, but rather reflects how well you would perform on a good day against a scratch player. (A scratch player has a handicap of zero and will shoot around par on a good day, depending on the course.) The formula used to compute handicaps is more complex than you'd care to know, but here is how the system basically works:

Every course is assigned a number of *course ratings,* one for each set of tees, by the local golf association. Check a scorecard; they're usually printed there. The total course rating is usually somewhere around par and indicates what a scratch golfer should shoot, all things considered, on a good day. A course's yardage and various obstacles, such as water hazards, are taken into account when calculating its total rating. The tougher the course, the higher its rating. For example, the Padre course at Camelback in Phoenix, Arizona, is just over sixty-five hundred yards with few hazards and wide fairways. Its course rating from the championship tees is 69.8. Down the road a few miles at Troon North, however, the course is over seven thousand

The Scorecard

Course yardage by hole	BLUE COURSE 73.0/136	372	196	530	422	125	309	516	197
	WHITE COURSE 71.9/129	472	185	515	418	120	364	500	155
	RED COURSE 73.7/135	420	160	490	368	85	390	460	135
	MEN'S PAR	5	3	5	4	3	4	5	3
	HANDICAP	9	11	1	7	17	15	3	13
Players' names									
Hole numbers	HOLE	1	2	3	4	5	6	7	8
Players' names									
	LADIE'S PAR	5	3	5	4	3	4	5	3
	HANDICAPE	9	13	1	3	17	11	5	15
	DATE						SCORER		

yards and dives in and out of complex rock formations; the course rating is 73.1, meaning that a scratch player would have more difficulty scoring there than on the Padre course.

Essentially what the handicap system does is select the best of your recent scores and apply them against the course rating to compute your handicap. If, for example, you've played ten times at Troon North in the last month, and your scores have ranged from 92 to 101, the handicap system throws out your eight highest scores and takes your 92 and next-lowest score— say, 95. The actual formula is more complex, but it basically subtracts the course rating, 73.1, from the mean of your two scores, 93.5. The resulting number, 20.4, is your handicap index. **Your index is not your handicap.** Your index is what helps you determine your handicap at whatever course you're playing. Using yet another formula called the *Slope System* (more on this later), each course has a conversion chart that lets you know how many strokes you are allotted against par, based on your handicap index. With a 20.4 index, you'd probably be allotted twenty-two or twenty-three strokes against par, depending on the course's difficulty. This would be your handicap. If the course is par 72, you'd be expected to shoot 94 or 95. Your index does not change from course to course; your handicap does.

The purpose of all this mathematics is to give players of various abilities the opportunity to play with each other and compete on an equal level. If a mid-80s player (say, 13.0 index) were to play with a mid-90s player (23.0 index), they would first check the conversion chart at whatever course they were playing to determine their handicaps—say, 15 and 26, respectively. The mid-80s player would then spot the mid-90s player the difference between their handicaps, or eleven strokes. It's like giving one player a head start, and, everything else being equal, makes for enjoyable, competitive matches most of the time. An added bonus: Handicaps not only bring players of all different abilities together, they give each individual player a system to chart his or her progress in the game.

Now, here's an interesting problem: Dave and Pete are golf buddies and play regularly at the Padre course at Camelback. Dave shoots in the mid-70s and has an index of 5.0. Pete shoots in the high 80s and has an index of 14.0. At Padre, Dave has a 5 handicap and Pete a 15, so Dave ordinarily spots Pete ten strokes. Suppose, however, they decide to play a round at the much more difficult Troon North. Would it be fair for Dave and Pete to play with that same ten-stroke differential?

No. It's wrong to assume that the tougher course would cost Pete the same number of strokes as Dave. A more likely scenario: Dave shoots 78, three strokes above his average, and Pete shoots 98, about nine strokes above his average. Why? Because the average player, who doesn't hit the ball all that far or consistently straight, is far more affected by a tough course's obstacles than a better player, so it's logical to assume that Pete will be thrown off his game more than Dave.

Which brings us to a discussion of *slope*. Slope is another number based on calculations of a course's difficulty, and is said to be more thorough than the course rating, taking into account such considerations as prevailing winds, changes in elevation, bunkers, rough, and trees. The idea behind slope, a relatively new concept, is to assess a course's difficulty based on the average, rather than scratch, golfer. Slope numbers range from 55 to 155, and the average slope rating is 113. Here's the way it works:

The Padre course, where Dave and Pete play, has a slope rating of 117, close to average, so each would get the same number of strokes as his index (5 and 14). The slope rating at Troon North is a whopping 146, however. Dave would likely get six or even eight strokes there, while Pete might get between eighteen and nineteen, thereby allowing for the fact that Troon North will be much more of a shock to Pete's system than

Dave's. Each course has a slope conversion chart that tells you how many strokes you're allotted, based on your index. If the course is easy and the slope rating is well under 113, be prepared to receive fewer strokes than your index. Conversely, if it's difficult, with a high slope rating, you'll receive more strokes.

What does it mean to "get strokes?" It *doesn't* mean that if you have a 10 handicap you're entitled to pick ten shots that you don't count during the round. Handicaps are to be used in one of two ways: In *stroke play,* in which you add all the strokes taken on each hole to produce a final score for the round, you subtract your handicap from that gross number to produce an adjusted, or net, score. So, if you shoot 81 and you're getting ten strokes, your net score will be 71. In *match play*, however, you play your opponent hole-by-hole: Whoever gets the lowest score on the current hole gets a point. In this case the player with the lower handicap gets no strokes, and the one with the higher gets the difference between the two handicaps. If Dave is a 5 and Pete a 14, Dave "gives" Pete nine strokes. But Pete doesn't get those nine wherever he chooses. Pete is given a one-stroke cushion on the nine toughest holes on the course, which have been determined by the course-rating team and printed on the scorecard. The number-1 handicap hole on the course is the toughest, the number-2 is the second toughest, all the way down to the number-18 handicap, which is the easiest. On each of the nine toughest holes, if Pete scores one stroke higher than Dave, the hole is a draw, or a *halve*. If they tie, Pete wins. Dave can only win if he scores two or more strokes better. On the remaining nine holes—the nine easiest—Dave and Pete play even.

So, now that you know what a handicap really is, how do you go about getting yourself one? If you belong to a private club or play at a particular course regularly, it's easy. Tell the pro-shop staff that you'd like to sign up to get a handicap, and for a small fee you'll be entered into the handicap system. From then on, you report every score you shoot, including those received at other courses. After your first five scores, you get a handicap. If you play at a number of courses regularly, pick one to record your scores. Which one is up to you; it will make no difference as far as your handicap is concerned.

If there are no courses you play regularly or your home course does not subscribe to the handicap system (very rare), seek out a public course that does. You don't have to play the course that records your handicap. Play wherever you like, keep track of your scores and the courses' ratings and slopes, then enter them en masse when you can make the trip to your "handicap course." For more information on the handicap system, contact the United States Golf Association at Golf House, Far Hills, NJ 07931.

CHAPTER 10

GOLFING MINORITIES

As is the case with many things in life, women and children who want to take up golf have a few extra obstacles to clear: namely, the men who don't make the game as accessible as it should be.

A search of most golf courses or pro shops for specialized programs or equipment for women or juniors will clearly deliver the message that golf is a game played primarily by men. This inequity may have been born from a pervasive this-is-man's-work attitude, but it survives today for financial reasons more than any others. Golf magazines, for example, rarely run instruction articles directed at women or juniors because less than 10 percent of their readers are women and even fewer are juniors; they have advertisers to think about. The other side of the argument, of course, is that if they ran more articles for women and juniors, more would read the magazine, which would generate more interest in the game. It's a bit of a catch-22.

WOMEN

Interestingly enough, statistics reveal that the number of women who try their hands at the game has been increasing rapidly year-to-year. The downside is that more women give up the game (or decide not to continue) than men. The reasons aren't completely clear. One thing's for sure: It's not because golf is inherently a man's game. More likely, the women who decide golf isn't for them have been given a less-than-pleasant introduction: restricted tee times, a lack of playing partners, lessons from husbands rather than teaching professionals. It's a rough road.

However, it can be negotiated. You can ensure that your initial exposure to the game is more than bearable by being smart and planning ahead. Women should keep the following things in mind after they've decided to take up the game:

Husbands are for marrying, not for golf lessons. The fastest way for you to become disenchanted with both the game and certain aspects of your relationship is to put yourself in the hands of your husband (or boyfriend, as the case may be) when it comes to your golf game. There are a few reasons. First of all, anytime you throw a teacher/student relationship into what's supposed to be a partnership, you've got a potentially dangerous mix. Yes, yes, this a golf book, not a guide to healthy marriages, but the old cliché of husbands and wives breaking up over golf exists, well, because it happens. This is not to suggest that taking golf lessons from your husband will end your marriage, but understand that learning the game can be a frustrating and humbling experience. You may get angry at your teacher at times, or feel resentful. It'll be much easier if the two of you don't have to go home together afterward.

There's a better reason, however, for not mixing marriage and golf instruction, and it falls more within this book's authority. Unless your husband, or boyfriend—or for that matter friend, male or female—is a PGA professional, he or she is not really cut out to teach you the game. He may have some knowledge of the fundamentals of the game, but communicating them to a beginner is a completely different matter. Teaching requires a keenly trained eye to spot the student's needs, and enough experience to prioritize those needs. Usually there are more than a few problems with your swing in the initial stages of your game, and only a teaching professional can know what to deal with first.

Be a discriminating consumer. This goes for all your choices: instruction, equipment, even the golf course you play. If you can, shop around, then look for the facilities that seem to have a more inclusionary attitude toward women. You'll get a good sense of the climate by walking into the pro shop. It's unlikely that the shop will stock as much women's equipment as men's, but there should be a solid selection. If you see a bunch of men's clubs and only a token women's set in the corner, you've got a pretty good indication that women do not have a strong presence at the club. It may be one to avoid. Here's why:

It's great to find a group of friends you can play with on a regular basis. But as a beginning golfer, you need to be able to go to the course without having to completely rely on a group of companions to join you each time. As social as golf can be, the game is truly an individual one, so you must have the opportunity for some independent discovery. It's vital, then, you find a course that won't make you feel like an illegal alien if you show up alone. Ask a few questions in the pro shop about how much female presence exists at the course: if there's a ladies' organization, if tee times are unrestricted, and so on. You'll quickly get a good idea of how friendly or hostile the environment is. Don't patronize a course that won't give you value for your hard-earned money.

You need to be just as discriminating when it comes to equipment. If you're looking for a set of clubs, your selection process should be just as thorough as any man's; that is to say, don't just settle for the token women's set in the corner. Follow the guidelines for buying equipment outlined in Chapter 4. Just make sure, wherever you go, that there is a substantial selection of women's clubs, as well as a PGA pro to assist you; and make sure that you're fitted properly and have the opportunity to test the clubs before you buy. Whatever you do, don't settle for a set of men's clubs unless you're physically very strong. Women's clubs are designed with more flexible shafts that allow them to perform when swung with less force.

Isolation is different, not necessarily better. "Specializing in women's golf" often means programs for women only, such as golf schools where all the students are women—and sometimes the instructors, too. The John Jacobs Schools (see Chapter 8), for instance, offer a few such programs. It's a common practice; in order to make women feel more "comfortable" as they learn or play the game, programs are set up so they can do so in the company of other women. It's the birds-of-a-feather theory, and it's well intentioned, but it isn't automatically the best way for you. True, you don't want to go anywhere you have to educate people about equality; but this doesn't mean you can't thrive in a mostly male environment. It's largely up to your individual needs. Your game won't necessarily suffer if you are one of a few women at a predominantly male golf school; in fact, there's a good chance that you'll get a lot out of the mix. The same goes for playing partners. It's assumed that if you're a woman, you need women friends to play with. Not necessarily. Whatever you're comfortable with is right. If you'd rather play with women, fine. But there's no rule that says this is the best thing for your game—or psyche, for that matter. Playing with men, if you're comfortable with it, can help raise the stakes of every round and ultimately make you a better golfer. By the way, this works the opposite way, too: Men don't need to isolate themselves with men only in the interest of their game. Golfers are golfers first, and men or women second. No matter who you play with, you can get something out of the experience: good swing mechanics to watch, different shots to play, interesting clubs in the bag, not to mention all the personal qualities your partners possess. Isolating yourself by gender really limits your opportunities.

JUNIORS

I assume that if you're reading this section, you have a youngster whom you'd like to introduce to golf, or who is asking you to do so. Either way, this is an opportunity to cherish, especially if you plan on making golf a part of your own life. Few pastimes are more rewarding than enjoying an early evening round of golf with your son or daughter. Even if you're both lousy. The companionship in a natural, outdoor environment is what will make the experience. Good golf from either player is just gravy.

That said, understand that some children will find golf not frenetic enough for their tastes. This is natural, and it's important to honor those feelings. You may think golf would be the best thing you could give your children; you may even think they could be the next Jack Nicklaus or Beth Daniel. If they

don't feel like playing, however, don't force it on them. If you're dying to have them play and they resist, settle for exposing them to the game with the trickle-down effect: The more you play, the more exposure they'll receive, which may eventually make them curious enough to give it a shot. It will be on their own terms, and that's important. When you introduce a youngster to the game—anyone, for that matter—it's vital that they not remember the experience as something they were dragged to. Such feelings will stay with them, and prevent them from enjoying the game fully.

So, wait for the green light before throwing your children into a junior golf program. Once they've shown an interest, then you can proceed. Here are a few things to keep in mind as you go:

Fathers are for fathering. . . Yes, the same rule applies here: Don't take it upon yourself to be your children's swing guru. Juniors, because they are generally far more instinctual than adults, need to be taught in a manner that's simpler than the instruction you'll probably receive. Spend as much time as you want with your children on the golf course, the range, the putting green, whatever, but leave the bulk of their instruction to a PGA professional. And shop carefully. You want your children to learn from a teacher who's very comfortable working with them—not all are—and will make the experience an enjoyable one.

Golf camps are for learning more, not simply learning. One of the best ways for juniors to learn more about the game is to attend a golf camp, a junior version of a golf school (described in Chapter 8). But "learning more" are the operative words here. Golf camps—where children spend four to eight hours a day playing, practicing, and studying golf—are for juniors who've already expressed strong interest in the game. As an introduction to the game, a camp may very well be too much of a toss into the deep end. In the beginning, less is more. Book one lesson for your children; if they like it, book another. Only after they start getting truly enthusiastic about the game should you consider a camp.

Seven Special Golf Camps: As in golf schools, a few qualities are constant from camp to camp: lots of golf, good instruction, some nongolf activities, a golf course, and so on. There are golf camps all over the country; they usually run in the summer and generally take children from ten to seventeen years old, although there are some exceptions. For a complete listing of the country's golf camps for juniors, again your source is Shaw's *Guide to Golf Schools and Camps*. However, the following seven camps deserve special mention because they offer programs specifically designed for your child *and you*. That's right, the two of you, learning the game together. It's a great opportunity for the two of you to experience something on the same level, because you will be students first and relatives second. The bonding potential will be high.

> **1. The Academy of Golf at PGA National Resort** —Mike Adams, director; 1000 Avenue of the Champions, Palm Beach Gardens, FL 33418; (800) 832-6325.
> **2. Arnold Palmer Golf Academy**—Tracy Dent, director; 9000 Bay Hill Boulevard, Orlando, FL 32819; (800) 523-5999, ext. 624.
> **3. Falcon Youth Golf Camp**—Richard L. Skimin, director; Dutchess Community College, 53 Rendell Road, Poughkeepsie, NY 12601 1595; (914) 471-4500, ext. 3506.
> **4. *Golf Digest* Instruction Schools**—John Hobbins, director; 5520 Park Avenue, Box 395, Trumbull, CT 06611 0395; (800) 243-6121.
> **5. Indiana Golf Academy**—Steve Bonnell, director; 711 West Norway Road, Monticello, IN 47960; (800) 972-9636.

6. Pine Needles Golfaris & Learning Center Golf Schools—Peggy Kirk Bell, director; P.O. Box 88, Southern Pines, NC 28388; (919) 692-7111.

7. Rocky Mountain Family Golf School—Ollie Woods, director; P.O. Box 456, Gunnison, CO 81230; (800) 758-RMGS.

Junior Golf Programs and Competition: Many courses, public and private, have junior golf programs designed to provide kids a place to learn and play the game with other kids. A typical junior golf program meets once a week during the summer months and is usually run by the PGA professional at the local course. A morning clinic, spent discussing various instructional topics, is often followed by one-on-one instruction, then perhaps a 9-hole tournament. At the end of the summer, all the participants play in a season-culminating tournament in which the program's junior champion is crowned.

Some programs are more intensive than others, but you'll find that most if not all include competition in their curriculum. Beginning adult golfers might find the idea of competing so early in their golf careers intimidating, but it's great experience for juniors, even if they're novices. In junior golf, the old saying "It's not whether you win or lose, it's how you play the game" is particularly true. Regardless of how they stack up next to the competition, playing in a tournament helps juniors set specific goals for themselves (golf is, after all, an individual game), and is also a great—and fast—way for them to get acquainted with rules and etiquette, which are always high on the priority list of most junior programs.

Kids Go Through Golf Clubs Like Shoes: You grimace when your eleven-year-old comes home from school and announces that he *must* have the new $130 pair of Nike basketball shoes. The price is bad enough; knowing that his toes are going to be sticking out the end of the shoes in three months makes this buy truly impractical.

Consider yourself lucky that golf clubs aren't the adolescent status symbol of choice—yet. You'll be in good shape if you spend less than $200 on a good set of junior-sized clubs with a bag, and, during those growth years, clubs bought to fit at Christmastime may be too small by the time the weather gets warm. The solution to this problem is simple: Don't buy clubs to fit. Yes, the clubfitting process for adults needs to be precise: a few misadjustments one way or another and you're bound to breed some really bad habits into your game. And, to be sure, it would be advantageous if your children could play with clubs that fit them perfectly all the time. But it's not very realistic. Juniors' swings have a way of being much more malleable than adults', and kids have the ability to adjust to clubs as their bodies change. So they won't be as adversely affected if their clubs are an inch too long or a bit too heavy.

Which clubs you buy your children depends mostly on their size and strength. There are basically five different categories of junior golfers, all with different equipment needs. Every child grows differently, of course, but here is a general outline to follow:

Tot (0-5 years old)—Search hard enough and you'll find miniature golf clubs made for children this age. If so, fine. But the traditional method of equipping these precocious ones is to cut down the shaft of a regular adult club and let them whack around the ball with it. This isn't a bad idea, especially if they're just hitting balls and not ready to tackle a course yet. Give them a midiron, a wedge, a putter, and perhaps a wood. If you don't have any old clubs, ask your pro. He'll probably have some lying around, and be willing to cut them down to size for you.

Peewee (5-8)—There are basically two different sizes of junior clubs available. Once your children reach five or six and want to perhaps make their way out onto the course for a few holes, they're ready for the smaller-sized junior clubs. These may or may not be available at your local pro shop; if not, the pro can easily order a set—although this can take a long time— or you might try one of the large discount chains, such as Las Vegas Golf or Nevada Bob's. Usually these sets come with one wood, three or four irons (3, 5, 7, and sometimes 9), and a putter. This is a fine starter set. Your children will become a better golfers if they learn with less rather than more.

Sprite (8-12)—At this age, 9 or even 18 holes shouldn't be too daunting a physical task for your children, so they'll need a set of clubs that will support them through a round of golf. The larger-sized junior clubs are designed to be legitimate sets: They can really be played with, and they stand up to a bit of a beating. The standard set makeup is usually a 1- and 3-wood, 3-, 5-, 7-, and 9-irons, a wedge, and a putter. Occasionally, you can find junior sets with a full makeup of three woods and eight irons, but they're rare and not really necessary. Having eight clubs to choose from is plenty, and gives children a chance to learn how to be creative with their shots.

Junior (12-14)—Once your children hit five feet, junior clubs probably won't hold up under their developing strength, and while men's clubs may still be too big and heavy for them, the softer, slightly shorter shafts and lighter weight of ladies' clubs will be a good match. This means a full set of clubs: three woods, eight or nine irons, a sand wedge, and a putter. This is more clubs than in junior sets, and a larger, full-sized bag, but the advantage for the cost conscious is that while junior clubs are usually only available new, you can usually find high-quality used ladies' clubs at your local pro shop. Be sure to have your children test the clubs before you buy. Since the selection of ladies' clubs is much broader, they can choose a set they're comfortable with.

Young adult (14 and up)—Girls, because their growth spurt happens earlier, are generally ready for full sized clubs before boys, usually between the ages of twelve and fourteen. Once boys reach their growth period, usually around fourteen, they're ready for the transition into men's clubs. However, since both genders may continue growing for three more solid years, it's still not practical to custom-fit children. They should definitely test the clubs before you buy, but your wisest move is to ask your local pro which specifications will last for them over the long haul. It's important to find a set they can grow into yet still handle right away.

CHAPTER 11

THE ESSENTIAL GOLFER

You've decided to make golf a part of your life. This may mean nothing more than a weekly 9-hole round, which is fine, but it could be argued that much of the golf world will still be out there waiting for you to discover it. If you really want the full experience, there are things you should do or see. A number of them, in no particular order, follow. Consider this your golfer's wish list:

Play 36 holes in one day. The final round of the U.S. Open used to be 36 holes. It's an all-day event, and it's exhausting. But, like a big holiday dinner, it's pure delight while you're in the middle of it. You're only sorry afterward. Make a tee time for 8 A.M. and another for 1:30. Play your morning round, have lunch, then head back out for the afternoon round. If you really want to be a hero, walk the entire 36. It'll do great things for your game, if not your feet.

Learn club repair. You can save a lot of money by learning basic repairs: changing grips, shortening or lengthening shafts, or changing the whipping thread that wraps around the neck of wooden clubs. What's more, it's a rewarding hobby, especially if you graduate to more advanced repair work, like refinishing or restoring wood and iron heads. For more information, check out *Golf Club Design, Fitting, Alteration, and Repair,* written by the guru of club repair, Ralph Maltby. His company, GolfWorks, sells all the materials you'll ever need. Contact it at (800) 848-8358.

Start a golf library. Educational value aside, good golf books have a way of being timeless reads. Aside from *First Tee,* of course, here a few to start with:

Jack Nicklaus's *Golf My Way* This is undoubtedly the best book of general golf instruction ever written—clear, understandable, and revealing—by undoubtedly the best golfer ever to play the game.

***Grand Slam Golf,* by George Peper** *Golf Magazine*'s editor-in-chief takes you inside the front gate—and the history books—of the greatest golf courses to have hosted major championships. Thoughtfully written and exquisitely photographed, this is a worthy addition to the finest of coffee tables.

Golf in the Kingdom, by Michael Murphy Now a cult classic: A young writer journeys to Scotland, and, with the help of an unusual Scottish pro named Shivas Irons, discovers the mystical connection between golf and life.

Dead Solid Perfect, by Dan Jenkins One of the few worthwhile fiction books about golf, **D.S.P.** chronicles the life of a PGA Tour pro as he battles fellow competitors, bed partners, and inner demons. Made into an HBO movie starring Randy Quaid.

The Little Red Book, by Harvey Penick Thoughts, concepts, philosophies, and anecdotes from the late teacher of Tour pros Ben Crenshaw and Tom Kite. The best selling sports book of all time.

The Golf Swing, by David Leadbetter with John Huggan As far as technical swing manuals go, there's none more logically put together. Nick Faldo's teacher explains his theories of a sound golf swing with clear, understandable language and precision color illustrations.

Subscribe to a golf magazine. This is the best way to stay up to date on all the goings on in the world of golf. There are a handful of magazines out there, but only three deliver consistently good material: *Golf Magazine, Golf Digest,* and *Golf World. Magazine* and *Digest* are monthlies and are instructionally driven, although features, equipment, and travel are well represented. Nothing offers more comprehensive coverage of the game, but be warned: Make either of them your instructional manual and your game will go south. (There's no substitute for a real teacher.) *Golf World,* on the other hand, is a weekly news magazine that covers the competitive world of golf. *World* features coverage of the pro and amateur tours, player profiles, as well as up-to-the-moment news stories. Because it's a weekly, it's the source for breaking stories in the golf world. Unparalled in writing quality and coverage.

Golf Magazine, subscriptions: (800) 876-7726.

Golf Digest, subscriptions: (800) 727-4653.

Golf World, subscriptions: (800) 627-4438.

Play 9 holes by yourself at sundown. You'll have the course, the trees, the shadows, and the sunset to yourself. Perhaps the most peaceful feeling you'll ever have.

Watch four days of Masters coverage. This would have been entitled GO SEE THE MASTERS, but that's kind of like saying, "Go have lunch with the president." Masters tickets are extremely difficult to get, but, luckily for all of us, television coverage of the first of golf's four "major" championships is excellent. Thursday's and Friday's rounds are broadcast on cable, usually the USA network; Saturday's and Sunday's rounds are traditionally broadcast on CBS. If you can't be at the Augusta National in the flesh, you'll get a good picture of it on the small screen. It's probably the most finely manicured golf course in the world— players have been said to be afraid to take divots there—with some of the most beautiful floral arrangements you'll see. But the highlight, of course, is the golf. The final 7 holes provide numerous opportunities for both glory and disaster, allowing dramatic lead changes to occur at any moment. Slow and steady golf doesn't win at Augusta—heroism does. Spend four days with the tournament and you'll never think golf on TV is boring again.

Go to a Tour event. You may not be able to get tickets for the Masters, but you shouldn't have any problem with any other tournament on the PGA, LPGA, or PGA Seniors Tour, even the U.S. Open. TV does not do justice to the incredible ability of the best players in the world. It's one thing to hear that John Daly just hit a 350-yard drive; it's quite another to stand next to him while he does it. You'll be blown away. Two of the best times during the week to attend: Tuesday, when most of the players play practice rounds, is much less crowded than subsequent

Go to a Tour event.

days, and the players are more relaxed, so it's a little easier to get close to them; and Sunday, which is very crowded, but gives you the opportunity to enjoy the electricity of a pressure-filled final round. If you have a favorite player, and you don't mind doing a lot of walking, follow him or her for the entire 18 holes. Watching a top pro manage his or her game over the course of a round will be very educational. For more information on tickets and tournaments in your area, contact the PGA Tour and PGA Senior's Tour at (904) 285-3700, the LPGA Tour at (407) 624-8400.

Take a golf vacation. Devoting your vacation time to seeking out golf destinations can be an extremely rewarding way to see the country, if not the world. A golf vacation doesn't necessarily mean 36 holes a day (although it can), but rather planning your itinerary around a daily round at one of a number of area courses. Some of the more popular destinations:

> **Orlando, Florida**—call the Florida Department of Commerce, Bureau of Visitor Services, at (904) 487-1462 for more information.

Myrtle Beach, South Carolina—call Myrtle Beach Golf Holiday, (800) 845-4653.

Hilton Head, South Carolina—call the Hilton Head Chamber of Commerce, (803) 785-3673.

Hawaii—call Real Hawaii, (800) 367-5108.

Northwest Michigan—call the Michigan Travel Bureau, (800) 543-2937.

Cape Cod, Massachusetts—call the Massachusetts Office of Travel and Tourism, (617) 727-3201.

Scottsdale, Arizon—call the Arizona Golf Association, (602) 953-5990.

Vail, Colorado—call the Colorado Golf Association, (303) 779-4653.

Austin, Texas—call the Texas Department of Highways and Public Transportation, Travel and Information Division, (800) 888-8839.

There's more. For a complete listing, check out *Golf Magazine,* which runs an annual ranking of the best resorts in America every November. It can be reached at (212) 779-5000.

See the Monterey Peninsula. The ultimate golf vacation: If such a thing exists, it surely happens here, on this magical stretch of California coastline. Monterey is about two hours from San Francisco, and it's home to two of the most beautiful and famous courses in the world, Cypress Point and Pebble Beach. Cypress Point is virtually inaccessible unless you know a member, but Pebble can be played by anyone, although you'll find it much easier if you're staying at the Pebble Beach Lodge or the nearby Inn at Spanish Bay. Pebble's first 5 holes are sleepers, but the 6th through 10th offer the most dramatic string of 5 holes in the game. All are situated on cliffs high above the Pacific Ocean, and give you the unmistakable feeling that you're playing golf at the edge of the world. Holes 11 through 17 return inland; then it's back to the rocky cliffs for the 18th, the quintessential finishing hole, which requires you to hit your

The 16th Hole at Cypress Point

drive over the Pacific to a coastline fairway.

Two other courses, Spyglass Hill and the Links at Spanish Bay, are also owned by the Pebble Beach Company and open to the public. Although not as famous as Pebble or Cypress, they offer stunning coastline golf as well. As for Cypress Point, you may not get a chance to play it, but you can see it—an experience in itself—by taking a drive along Seventeen Mile Drive, the road that encases the peninsula. Pull over by the 15th tee and take a look at perhaps the most picturesque par-3 in the world. Look closely and you'll see sea lions playing on the rocks below the green.

For more information, contact central reservations at Pebble Beach, (800) 654-9300.

Play a top-fifty course. If it's difficult for you to conceptualize what makes a great course great (hint: it's not just well manicured grass), you'll immediately understand when you step onto one of the best courses in the world. They're tougher, prettier, and capture your imagination in ways an average course won't. If you get a chance to play any of them, jump at it. And bring lots of golf balls.

Each year, the two major golf magazines, *Golf Magazine* and *Golf Digest,* publish a ranking of the 100 best golf courses in the world. Most of the top fifty—Pine Valley, Cypress Point, Augusta National—are private clubs, inaccessible to the average Joe (unless you happen to be good friends with a member). There are, however, two exceptions:

> **Pebble Beach Golf Links.** Ranked number three in the United States and the world by *Golf Magazine.* See above.
>
> **Harbor Town Golf Links.** Famous for its distinctive red-and-white lighthouse next to the 18th green, Harbor Town is part of the Sea Pines resort on Hilton Head Island, South Carolina, and can be played as part of a guest package at the resort. Ranked forty-second in the

world and twenty-fourth in the U.S.

Your other option is to travel overseas and play in the British Isles, where many of the greatest courses are accessible to any golfer. Which leads us to the next item on the list:

Play golf in Scotland and/or Ireland. All golfers should have the opportunity to experience golf as it was played during its early years, before it came to America. Luckily, in many ways the game hasn't changed much in the British Isles. Some of the greatest golf courses in the world—St. Andrews, Royal Troon, Ballybunion, Portmarnock—uphold the same values and traditions that allowed the game to flourish in the seventeenth century. They are all accessible to the public (although some advance planning is usually required), and offer a peek at what golf was meant to be when it was invented: a game for the common man, played over completely natural terrain, in any kind of weather. That is golf in Ireland and Scotland. Many of the courses are built right next to the sea, rolling in and around sand dunes and over linksland. In one round, you could experience high winds, rain, and sleet. On the other hand, it could remain warm and sunny for the entire round. You just never know. It's a different type of game than is played in the States, but there's a good chance you'll like it better. Not because of the caddy who knows every inch of the course, or even the ale you quaff at the local pub after the round. But because you're in the home of the game, and you'll feel that way. For more information, contact:

> Mark Rigg, **Links Golf St. Andrews,** 7 Pilmour Links, St. Andrews Fife, Scotland KY16 9JG; (011) (44) 334-478639.

> **Ireland Golf Tours,** 251 East 85th Street, New York, NY 10028; (800) 346 5388.

Hit a persimmon driver. Just to know what it feels like, since these clubs are increasingly rare. Persimmon was the material of choice for woods until the eighties, when metal began to take over. You'll find a persimmon driver less forgiving of off-center hits, but, as with a baseball bat, there's a satisfaction that comes with a solid wooden wood shot that metal can't duplicate. Traditionalists will tell you that the best persimmon woods were made in the late forties and fifties, when MacGregor offered its Tommy Armour, Toney Penna, and Tourney lines. Today, although they're collector's items, they continue to find their way into a number of Tour pros' bags. These clubs feature distinctive mahogany stains that reveal persimmon's naturally flowing grain, and often contain multicolored fiber inserts in the hitting area. If you can get your hands on one, don't let go. For more information on collectible golf clubs, contact **American Golf Classics,** in Newport News, Virginia, at (804) 874-7271.

Learn the pro moves. Good golf is largely about self-confidence, and nothing boosts self-confidence more than the feeling that you know what you're doing—or at least look like you do. Developing a pro swing or putting stroke may be a tall order, but there are a lot of other things pros do on the golf course that you can pick up fairly quickly:

A persimmon wood

The pro tee Very important, especially on the first tee where a number of people may be watching. Hold the tee between the middle and ring fingers of your right hand, with the ball in your palm. Standing so your left shoulder faces the fairway, bend over so you are supporting yourself with your left leg only, and place the tee in the ground. When you open your hand, the ball should stay on the tee. The more professional you are, the more this is one fluid motion.

Money marks Pros never use plastic ball-markers on the green. They only use coins, and usually only pennies and dimes, because they're small and thin. Nickels and quarters are too big and bulky, although marking your ball with a New York City subway token (a little thinner than a nickel) is pretty cool.

Proper glove etiquette A major measuring stick of pro-ness. Never wear your golf glove when you putt, because that superthin layer of leather will decrease some of the feel in your hand. When a pro takes off his or her glove, he carries it like a baseball player does: The palm of the glove goes in the right rear pocket, and the fingers hang out. To really take care of your glove, take it off between full shots, especially on hot days. This will prevent the glove from soaking up sweat, increasing its life span.

Tend the pin like a pro When a playing partner asks you to tend the pin for him on a long putt, do it like the pro caddies do: Grasp the flagstick from the top so your hand closes around the flag itself, preventing it from flapping in the wind. Briefly lift up the flagstick an inch to make sure it isn't stuck in the hole at the bottom of the cup, and be sure to stand so your shadow doesn't cross the hole.

Practice tee conservation You're hitting on a driving

range with a grass tee. You whack a 7-iron and take a divot. Where do you place the next ball? If you're like most amateurs, you'll put it at the front of the divot hole to give yourself the feeling that the ball is teed up. But if you have pro moves, you'll put the ball just behind the back of the divot hole. Why? It saves grass. If you hit your next shot solidly, you won't cut an entire new divot, you'll just take out that small sliver of turf between the ball and the old divot hole.

Carry a real towel Those flimsy golf towels they sell in pro shops don't stand up to all the needs of a pro. Since pros never use the ball washers on the course, you'll need a towel that's big enough to keep half of it wet (to clean balls and clubs) and the other half dry (to wipe hands and grips). Get a decent-sized towel that has real absorbency. And make it white, or at least a solid color. No prints for the pros.

Start a putter collection Ask a pro what he looks for in a putter and he'll probably say that he likes a putter that makes putts. With a couple of twelve-footers standing between him and millions of dollars, can you blame him? And since humans are fickle animals, you can't really blame him for having an array of putters to choose from, either, just in case the one he's using isn't "behaving." It's not a bad thing to indulge yourself the same way. You don't need a bagful of putters, but having a few of different shapes, sizes, and weights can help you. Because it is so feel-oriented, putting is very much an emotional activity, more so than the rest of your game. It's important, therefore, to be able to use a putter that fits your mood.

GLOSSARY

Ace. Hitting the ball into the hole on the first stroke of a hole. Also known as a *hole in one.*

Address. Positioning of the body and club in preparation for a stroke.

Approach. A shot played to the putting green of a hole. *Approach shot* usually refers to a full swing made with the intention of the ball finishing on the green.

Apron. A grass area surrounding the putting green, usually mowed longer than the green but shorter than the rough. Also known as *fringe.*

Away. The ball farthest from the hole when more than one ball is in play. It determines order of play: Whoever's ball is away plays first.

Back side. The second 9 holes of an 18-hole course, holes 10 through 18. Also known as the *back 9* or *inward half.*

Backspin. The reverse spin imparted to the ball by solid contact with the club; it causes the ball to rise in the air and stop when it hits the green.

Backswing. The initial half of the swing; it starts with the clubhead being on the ground and moving back away from the ball and over the head.

Ball in play. A ball is in play when the player has made a stroke on the teeing ground. It remains in play until the player holes out on that same hole, unless it gets lost, goes out of bounds, or is taken out of play in accordance with the rules.

Ball marker. An object—usually flat and round, like a coin—used to mark a ball's position on the putting green.

Bent grass. A type of grass used primarily in the cooler climates of the North.

Bermuda grass. A longer-grain grass used primarily in the warmer climates of the South.

Birdie. One stroke under the par of any hole.

Bite. Slang term for backspin; it's also used as an admonishment for the ball to stop quickly: "Bite!"

Blade. The clubhead of an iron, in particular a head made of forged carbon steel, because this is generally thinner and more sleek than cast. The term also refers to a thinner type of putter head.

Block. To swing in such a manner as to propel the ball in a straight line right of the target.

Bogey. One stroke over the par of any hole.

Bunker. An area of ground, usually sunken, like a pit, and covered or filled with sand. It's a hazard under the Rules of Golf, but does not exact a penalty if your ball finds it.

Caddie. A person hired to carry and handle a player's clubs during a round and help negotiate the ins and outs of the course.

Carry. The distance from where the ball is struck by the club to the spot it touches the ground for the first time.

Casual water. A temporary accumulation of water on the course in a place that ordinarily doesn't have it. Rain or melting snow can cause casual water; dew can't. The standard way to measure: If the water rises above the soles of your shoes when you step in it, it's casual water. Casual water is never a hazard; rather, the player is entitled to a free drop to drier ground.

Chip shot. A low-trajectory shot, usually hit around the green, designed to carry a short distance then roll toward the hole.

Choke down. To grip the club farther down on the handle, so the hands are nearer to the shaft.

Closed stance. For a right handed golfer, a position in which a line drawn across the tops of the feet points right of the target.

Closed clubface. For a right-handed golfer, a position in which the leading edge of the clubface points left of the target.

Clubhead. The part of the club used to hit the ball.

Clubhouse. A building at a golf course that usually has locker rooms, a restaurant, and a bar.

Course. The area of play, usually made up of 9 or 18 holes, each with a tee, fairway, and putting green.

Course rating. A number indicating the difficulty of a given course relative to others. Expressed in strokes and decimal points of strokes, it's used in computing a player's handicap under the United States Golf Association's handicap system. The higher a course's course rating, the more difficult it is.

Cup. See *hole*.

Dimple. Round indentations in the ball scientifically designed to steady its flight.

Divot. A piece of turf cut out by the club during a stroke.

Dogleg. A hole that bends to the right or left with an angle in the fairway.

Double bogey. Two strokes over the par of any hole.

Double eagle. Three strokes under the par of any hole. Also known as an *albatross*.

Draw. A shot that moves right-to-left in a controlled manner. It's the less severe and more desirable version of a hook. See *hook*.

Drive. The shot played from a tee.

Driver. Also known as the *1-wood;* it's usually used to hit off the teeing ground when maximum distance is desired.

Duck hook. A severe version of a hook. It travels low and hard and usually finishes well left of the target.

Eagle. Two strokes under the par of any hole.

Face. The hitting area of a golf club. Also known as the *clubface.*

Fade. A shot that moves left-to-right in a controlled manner. It's the less severe and more desirable version of a slice. See *slice*.

Fairway. The area of grass between the teeing ground and putting green of a hole, mowed shorter and kept better than the rough. It's designed to reward the accurate driver with a good lie for his or her second shot.

Fat shot. A stroke in which the club hits the ground before hitting the ball, causing a severe loss of power.

Finish. The final position of the swing, after the ball is on its way toward the target. See also *follow through*.

Flagstick. A marker placed in the hole to indicate its position from long distances. Also known as a *pin*.

Flier. A shot from the rough that leaves the clubface with reduced backspin, allowing it to ride wind currents and fly unusually far.

Follow-through. The portion of the swing that occurs after the ball has been struck.

Fore. A warning call to fellow golfers to beware of an approaching golf ball, from the British "look out before!"

Forecaddie. A person employed to mark the position of players' shots on the course. It's a relatively rare private club phenomenon.

Foursome. A group of four golfers playing together.

Fringe. See *apron*.

Gimme. A putt so short that it's conceded by a partner or opponent. *Gimme range* is usually within a foot of the hole.

Grain. The direction in which grass grows on a putting green.

Green. In the official Rules of Golf, *green* refers to the entire golf course; hence the terms *greens fee, greenskeeper,* etc. Popularly, however, *green* means the putting surface of a hole, marked by closely cut grass and a hole or cup with a flagstick.

Greens fee. The fee paid for the privilege of playing the golf course.

Grip. The section of the shaft, usually covered by rubber, that serves as a place to hold the golf club. The term also refers to the action itself of holding the club.

Ground under repair. An area on the course marked by the rules committee that is temporarily out of sorts, e.g., a patch of freshly planted seed. A player is allowed a free drop without penalty.

Handicap. The number of strokes a player receives to adjust his or her score to the level of a scratch or zero-handicap golfer.

Hazard. Two kinds: bunkers and water hazards. See *bunker*. Water hazards are brooks, streams, rivers, lakes, ponds, ditches, or any open bodies of water, full or empty, on the golf course. All ground or water within the boundaries of the hazard is part of the hazard. Water hazards are often marked by red lines or stakes, which are also part of the hazard.

Heel. The portion of the clubhead nearest the shaft. Shots hit from this portion of the face are also referred to as *heeled.*

Hole. A round receptacle in the green, 4-¼ inches in diameter and at least 4 inches deep, usually lined with metal. Also known as a *cup.* The term also refers to units of play on a golf course: 18 holes make up an entire course, and a round.

Hole in one. A hole made in one stroke. Also known as an *ace.*

Honor. The right to hit first from the tee, which goes to the lowest scorer on the previous hole, or, if there was a tie, to whomever had the most recent lowest score on a hole.

Hook. To hit a ball in a curve to the left of the intended target.

Hosel. The hollow part of the iron clubhead into which the shaft is fitted.

Insert. The hitting portion of the clubface of wooden clubs, usually made of plastic or fiber.

Iron. Clubs made with a smaller metal head, designed for accurate shots intended for the green. Irons are usually broken up into three classifications: *long irons* (1, 2, 3, 4), *midirons* (5, 6, 7), and *short irons* (8, 9, PW). As the numbers get higher, the face carries more loft and the shaft is usually shorter, resulting in more accuracy and less distance.

Lag. A longer putt intended to finish close to the hole to afford an easy second putt.

Lateral hazard. A water hazard that runs approximately parallel to the line of play on a hole.

Lie. The position in which the ball sits on the ground. The term also refers to the angle formed by the shaft and the ground when the clubhead is sitting in its natural position.

Line. The direction in which a player intends the ball to travel after it's been hit. Also known as *target line.*

Links. Originally used to describe a seaside golf course, the term now refers colloquially to any golf course.

Lip. The top edge or rim of the cup or hole.

Lob shot. A high-flying, soft-landing shot, usually hit with a wedge, designed to gain access to a pin that will not accept a rolling shot. It flies almost straight up then comes almost straight down, and is particularly helpful when there's a bunker between the ball the flagstick.

Loft. The angle at which the clubface is set from vertical; meant to lift the ball into the air.

Loose impediments. Natural objects that are not fixed or growing, including unembedded stones, twigs, leaves, and branches. These may be moved as long as their removal does not affect the position of the ball as it lies.

LPGA. The Ladies Professional Golf Association, the pro tour for women.

Match. A golf competition played by holes each hole is a separate contest rather than by total score. The team or player winning the greatest number of holes is the winner. *Match play* refers to this type of competition.

Medal play. A competition decided by total overall score, with every stroke counting and being significant. Also known as *stroke play.*

Mulligan. A second shot, or replay, often permitted from the first tee of a casual round, but strictly prohibited by the Rules of Golf.

Nassau. A popular form of competition, in either match or stroke play, in which a point is awarded to the winner of the first 9 holes, a point to the winner of the second 9, and a point to the overall 18-hole winner.

Net. A player's score after it has been adjusted using a handicap.

Open. A tournament open to both amateurs and professionals.

Open stance. A setup position in which the left foot is pulled away from the target line, so a line drawn across the tops of the feet would point left of the target.

Out of bounds. The ground outside the course, on which play is prohibited. Hitting a ball out of bounds requires a stroke penalty and a replay of the shot from the ball's original position.

Par. Golf's standard of good performance. The term refers specifically to the theoretical number of strokes a player should take for a hole.

Partner. A player associated with another player on the same side in a match.

Penalty stroke. A stroke added to a player's score for violation of a specific rule.

PGA. The Professional Golf Association.

Pin. See *flagstick.*

Pitch. A short shot to the putting green, characterized by a high arc and little roll.

Pitch and run. A pitch shot with a lower-lofted club, like an 8- or 9-iron, that has less backspin and therefore rolls upon hitting the green.

Pitching wedge. An iron designed primarily for making short pitch shots.

Playing through. Occurs when a group of players is allowed to pass the group in front of them.

Pro shop. A place to buy golf equipment, operated by the club professional.

Provisional ball. A second ball played if the original ball may be lost or out of bounds. It prevents walking back to the original spot if indeed a stroke-and-distance penalty is required.

Pull. A shot that flies left of the target in a fairly straight line.

Punch. A low, controlled shot hit with an iron. Useful to find headwinds, it's executed with a short, smashing-type swing.

Push. A shot that flies right of the target in a fairly straight line.

Putt. Stroking the ball toward the hole when on the putting surface.

Putter. A club with a flat, virtually unlofted face, used to roll the ball on the putting green.

Putting green. The area of each hole specially prepared for putting. It usually has the shortest and best-manicured grass on the course.

R&A. The Royal and Ancient Golf Club of St. Andrews, Scotland. It's the keeper of the European Rules of Golf.

Rough. Areas, usually bordering the green, fairway, and hazards, of longer grass designed to make solid contact difficult.

Run. The distance the ball rolls after hitting the ground.

Run-up. An approach shot that lands before the putting surface and rolls on, rather than landing on the green and staying there.

Sand trap. Colloquial expression for bunker. See *bunker.*

Sand wedge. An iron with a heavy flange on the bottom, designed primarily to extract the ball from greenside bunkers.

Scratch. To play at par. A *scratch player* receives no handicap.

Set. A full complement of golf clubs.

Shaft. The part of the club that is not the head.

Shank. To hit the ball on the hosel or neck of the club, causing it to veer off at a sharply right angle.

Short game. Made up of chipping, pitching, and putting.

Skull. A mis-hit shot, hit with an iron or wedge, in which the leading edge of the clubhead makes contact near the equator of the golf ball, resulting in a low, scooting shot.

Sky. A mis-hit shot, usually hit with a wood and a teed ball, in which the clubhead hits underneath the ball, sending it higher than intended. It's similar to a pop fly in baseball.

Slice. A shot that curves right of the target.

Sole. The bottom of the clubhead. The term also refers to the act of placing the club on the ground at the address.

Sole plate. A metal plate on the bottom of a wooden club.

Square clubface. A position in which the leading edge is perpendicular to the target line.

Square stance. A stance in which both feet are parallel to the target line.

Stance. The position of the feet when addressing the ball.

Stroke. Any forward motion of the club made with the intention of hitting the ball, whether successful or not.

Stroke play. See *medal play.*

Sweet spot. The point on the clubface at which the most-solid contact can be made—usually dead center.

Swing. The action of making a stroke.

Takeaway. The beginning of the backswing.

Tee. A wooden peg on which the ball is placed for the purposes of driving. The term also refers to the area from which drives are hit, and is also known as *teeing ground.*

Tee-marker. An object on the teeing area of a hole that marks the forwardmost point from which a drive can be played.

Threesome. A group of three golfers playing together.

Toe. The portion of the clubhead farthest from where it joins the shaft.

Top. To hit a ball above center, causing it to roll or hop rather than rise off the ground.

Tournament. A competition of either match or stroke play.

Trouble shot. A recovery stroke taken from a trouble position such as a bunker, rough, or behind trees.

Turn. The change from the front 9 to back 9. *Making the turn* is moving from the 9th green to 10th tee.

Unplayable lie. A ball in a position where it physically cannot be played, e.g., amid rocks or dense trees and shrubs.

USGA. The United States Golf Association.

Waggle. Before the actual swing, a flexing of the wrists that causes the club to swing back and forth.

Water hazard. See *hazard.*

Water hole. A hole on which a sizable amount of water comes into play.

Wedge. A high-lofted iron used for short shots.

Whipping. The thread wrapped around the neck of a wooden club, designed to prevent cracking.

Winter rules. Locally mandated rules that allow players to improve their lies in the fairway.

Wood. A club with a large head, made of wood or metal, designed to hit the ball long distances.

Yips. Convulsive shakes that cause a player to badly miss short putts.

INDEX

Academy of Golf at PGA
National Resort, 128
ace, 145
address, 145
albatross, 147
alignment, 42*illus.*, 43—44
All Clubs, One Target, 108
American Golf Classics, 142
approach shots, 19
apron, 145
Arnold Palmer Golf Academy,
128
away ball, 145

backside, 145
backspin, 55, 56, 145
backswing, 44, 46, 145
bag handlers, 66—67,
67*illus.*, 70
bags, 31
ball above/below feet, 56
ball in play, 145
ball marks, fixing, 84*illus.*,
86—87
ball position, 43
balls, 12, 31—32, 64, 79—80,
82—83
Ben Sutton Golf Academy,
102—103
bent grass, 145
Bermuda grass, 85, 145
birdie, 145
bite, 146
blades, 146
blocking, 146
Blue Monster, 103
body position, 41, 43
bogey, 146
books on golf, 134—135
bounce, 26, 28*illus.*, 54
bunker shots, 54—55
buying clubs, 29—31

caddies, 66, 68*illus.*, 68—70,
146
carry, 146
cash payment for services,
66, 70
casual water, 146
centrifugal force, 23, 25
children. *See* juniors, golf and
chip shots, 26, 48, 49*illus.*,

50, 101, 146
choke down, 146
closed clubface, 146
closed stance, 146
Closest to the Pin, 108
clothing, 35—36
clubhouses, 71, 146
clubs. *See* golf clubs
clubshafts, 27, 29
compression (of balls), 32
country clubs, 3, 4—5
course ratings, 116, 147
crosswinds, 56
Cypress Point course
(Monterey, California),
138, 140

Daniel, Beth, 126
Dave Pelz Short Game
School, 101—102, 109
Dead Solid Perfect (Jenkins),
135
delayedhit position, 46
distractions, 80
divots, 84*illus.*, 85, 147
Doral Golf Learning Center
with Jim McLean, 103
DoralRyder Open, 103
double bogey, 147
double eagle, 147
downhill lies, 57
downswing, 44, 46
Drawback, 109
dress code, 12—13, 35
drivers, 18, 22—23, 108, 112,
147
dropping, 90, 90*illus.*
duck hook, 147

electric carts, 13—14, 70
Eleven, 109—110
England, golf in, 4
equipment, 11—12, 21—23,
24—25*illus.*, 26—27,
28*illus.*, 29—36
etiquette, 73—93, 143

fairways, 19, 147
fairway woods, 23, 57
Falcon Youth Golf Camp, 128
Faldo, Nick, 135
fast play, rules of, 77—80

fathers, golf lessons from, 127
fat shots, 147
Faxon, Brad, 103
flagsticks, 19, 87, 148
putting and, 91—92
Flick, Jim, 101
followthrough, 44, 47, 148
footprints, 81, 86, 87
fore, 148
forecaddies, 148
forty-five-minute warm-up,
111—113
fringe, 19, 148

games for practice, 107—110
"getting strokes," 119
gimme, 148
gloves, 34—35, 64, 143
golf, origins of, 1, 2*illus.*,
3—6
golf camps, 127—129
*Golf Club Design, Fitting,
Alteration, and
Repair* (Maltby), 134
golf clubs, 11—12, 18—19,
22—23, 24*illus.*,
26—27, 28*illus.*,
29—31, 108, 112
for juniors, 130—132
repair of, 134
for women, 124—125
golf courses, 8, 15—16,
16—17*illus.*, 18—20,
61—62
getting around, 13—14
private courses, 66—70
public courses, 62—65
reservations, 10
resort courses, 70—71
in Scotland and Ireland,
141—142
taking care of, 84—87
top fifty (United States),
140—141
Golf Digest, 135
Golf Digest Instruction
Schools, 101, 128
Golf in the Kingdom
(Murphy), 135
Golf Magazine, 104, 134, 135
golf magazines, 96, 122,
135—136

Golf My Way (Nicklaus), 134
golf schools, 99—105, 125
Golf Swing, The
 (Leadbetter), 135
golf vacations, 137—138,
 139*illus.*, 140
Golf World, 135
Grand Slam Golf (Peper),
 134—135
grass, 16, 59, 86
greens, 18, 80—83, 148
greens fees, 13, 65, 66, 69, 71,
 148
greenside manners, 87
grip, 38*illus.*, 39—41, 148
grounding the club, 91
group lessons, 98—99
*Guide to Golf Schools and
 Camps* (Shaw), 104,
 128

halve, 119
handicaps, 115—120, 148
Harbor Town Golf Links
 (South Carolina),
 140—141
hats, 36, 64
having the honor, 89
hazards, 20, 148
head covers, 31
headwinds, 55—56
heel, 149
hilly lies, 56—57
hole in one, 149
hole numbers, 18
honor system, 74
Honourable Company of
 Edinburgh Golfers, 3
hook, 149
HORSE, 108—109
hosel, 149
Huggan, John, 135
husbands, golf lessons from,
 122—123

Indiana Golf Academy, 128
insert, 149
instruction, 96—105
interlock, 40
inward half, 145
Ireland, golf in, 4, 141—142
irons, 23, 26, 57, 108, 149

Jacobsen, Peter, 103
Jenkins, Dan, 135
John Jacobs Golf Schools,
 102, 125
juniors, golf and, 126—132

Kite, Tom, 103

Ladies Professional Golf
 Association, 150
ladies' tees, 18
lag, 149

lateral hazards, 149
Leadbetter, David, 135
lie, 149
links, 149
Links at Spanish Bay
 (Monterey, California),
 140
Little Red Book, The
 (Penick), 135
lob shots, 149—150
lob wedges, 26—27
locker rooms, 62*illus.*, 63,
 66—67, 71
loft, 23, 50, 54, 150
long irons, 26
loose impediments, 150
lost balls, 79—80
LPGA, 150
LPGA Tour, 137

Maltby, Ralph, 134
markers, 145
Masters coverage, 136—137
match play, 119
McLean, Jim, 103, 104
medal play, 150
mental factors, 55—59
midirons, 26
money marks, 143
Monterey Peninsula
 (California), golf in,
 138, 139*illus.*, 140
moving a mark, 82*illus.*, 83
Mulligan, 150
multiple club/cart trick, 77
municipal courses, 65
Murphy, Michael, 135

Nassau, 150
Nicklaus, Jack, 97, 101, 126
Nicklaus/Flick Golf Schools,
 101

oneonone lessons, 97—98
open stance, 150
out of bounds, 20, 150
overlap, 40

pace of play, 75—80
Padre course (Phoenix,
 Arizona), 116, 118
par for the course, 18
pars, 18, 150
Pebble Beach Golf Links
 (Monterey, California),
 68, 138, 140
Pelz, Dave, 109
penalties, 20, 54, 74, 83, 89,
 92
penalty strokes, 151
Penick, Harvey, 135
Peper, George, 134
persimmon drivers, 141*illus.*,
 142
PGA, 96, 97, 151

PGA of America, 97
PGA Seniors Tour, 137
PGA Tour, 97, 103, 137
pin, tending the, 143
Pinehurst Golf Advantage
 Schools, 103—104
Pine Needles Golfaris &
 Learning Center Golf
 Schools, 129
pitch and run, 151
pitching wedges, 26, 151
pitch shots, 26, 48, 49*illus.*,
 50, 101
playing partners, taking care
 of, 80—83
playing through, 151
practice greens, 63*illus.*, 105
practice swings, 78—79, 107
practicing, 105—110
preshot preparation, 78
private courses, 66—70
Professional Golfer's
 Association. *See* PGA
professionals, 9, 30, 97, 122,
 127
pro shops, 8, 13, 30, 32, 35,
 63—64, 119, 123
pro tees, 143
provisional ball, 151
public courses, 120
pullcarts, 13
punch shots, 151
putter collections, 144
putters, 27, 151
putting, 51*illus.*, 51—53, 101,
 109—110, 151

Ram, Drop, and Die, 110
Range Scorecard, 107—108
reading the green, 58—59
resort courses, 70—71
Rocky Mountain Family Golf
 School, 129
Ross, Donald, 104
rough, 19, 57, 151—152
Royal and Ancient Golf Club
 of St. Andrews, 3, 151
rules, 3, 5, 87—93
Rules of Golf, 79—80, 82, 91

St. Andrews Society of
 Golfers, 3
sand bunkers, 20, 91, 152
 raking, 84*illus.*, 85—86
sand explosion, 53*illus.*
sand play, 54—55, 101
sand traps. *See* sand bunkers
sand wedges, 26, 112, 152
scorecards, 116*illus.*
scoring, 79, 110
Scotland, golf in, 3—5, 65,
 141—142
scratch, 152
scratch players, 116
semiprivate courses, 69

setup, 41, 42*illus.*, 43—44, 52
shanking, 152
shirts, 35
shoes, 13, 32—34, 33*illus.*,
    63, 66—67, 81
short game, 101—102, 107,
    110, 152
short irons, 26
single golfers, 11
skull, 152
slice, 152
slope, 118
Slope System, 117
slow play, 75—78
speed, 9
sporting goods stores, 32
Spyglass Hill course
    (Monterey, California),
    140
square clubface, 152
starters, 64—65
stroke and distance penalty,
    89
stroke play, 88, 119

sweet spot, 24*illus.*, 153
swing, 44, 45*illus.*, 46—48

tailwinds, 56
tee box, 16
tee conversation, 143—144
teeing ground, 16, 18
teemarkers, 18, 89, 153
tee times, 10, 62—63, 69
    for women, 122, 124
ten basic rules of play,
    88—93
tenminute warmup, 113
tipping, 66, 67, 70
topfifty courses, 140—141
Tour events, 137
towels, 144
tree trouble, 57—58
Troon North course
    (Phoenix, Arizona),
    116—117, 118
trouble shots, 153
twosomes, 10

United States, golf in, 3—5
United States Golf
    Association. *See* USGA
uphill lies, 57
U.S. Open, 134
USGA, 5, 88, 93, 120, 153
utility woods, 23

Vardon grip, 40
videos, 96

waggle, 153
warming up, 111—113
water hazards, 20, 91
wedges, 26—27, 112, 153
wind, 55—56
winter rules, 153
women, golf and, 32,
    122—126
woods, 22—23, 108, 154

yips, 154